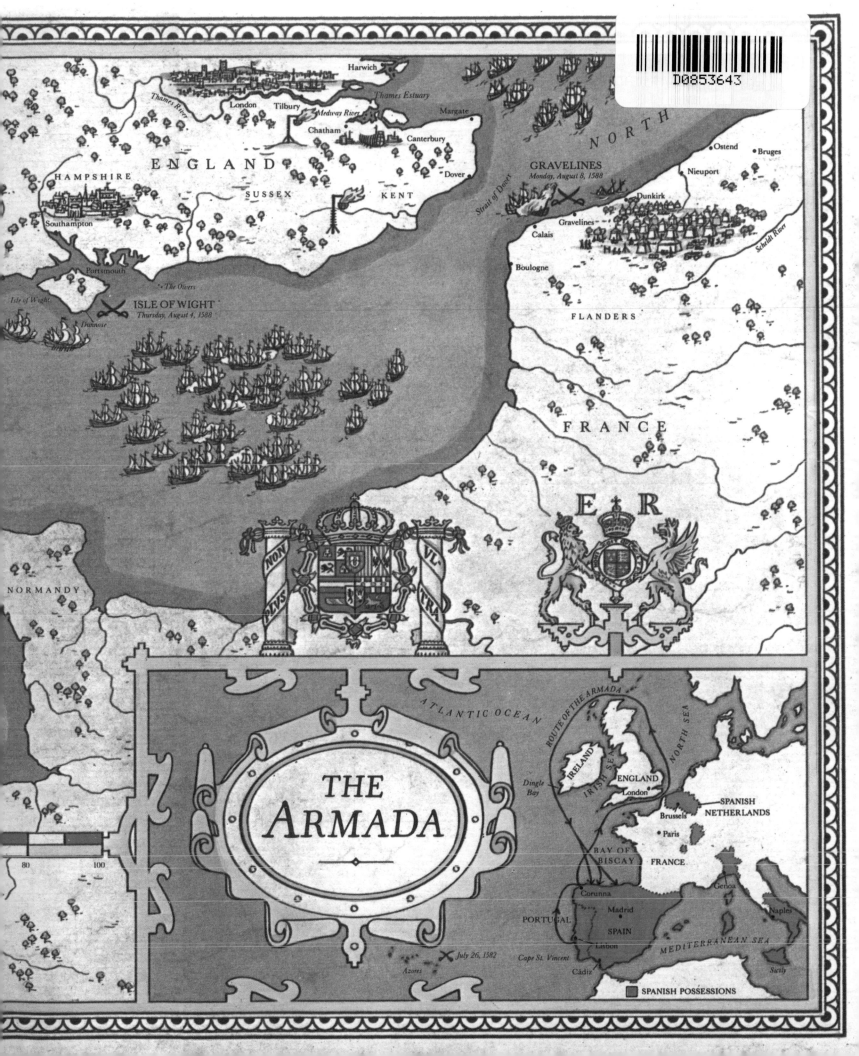

THE ARMADA

Harwich

Thames River

London Tilbury Medway River Thames Estuary Margate

Chatham

Canterbury

ENGLAND

Dover

HAMPSHIRE

SUSSEX KENT

Southampton

Portsmouth

The Oivers

Isle of Wight ISLE OF WIGHT
Thursday, August 4, 1588

Dunnose

NORMANDY

NORTH

GRAVELINES
Monday, August 8, 1588

Ostend Bruges

Nieuport

Strait of Dover

Dunkirk

Calais Gravelines

Boulogne Scheldt River

FLANDERS

FRANCE

E   R

NON VL·
PLVS TRA

ATLANTIC OCEAN

ROUTE OF THE ARMADA

NORTH SEA

IRELAND ENGLAND

IRISH SEA

Dingle Bay

London

SPANISH
NETHERLANDS

Brussels

Paris

BAY OF
BISCAY FRANCE

Genoa

80 100

Corunna

Madrid

Naples

PORTUGAL SPAIN

Lisbon MEDITERRANEAN SEA

× *July 26, 1582*

Azores Cape St. Vincent

Cádiz Sicily

■ SPANISH POSSESSIONS

The Seafarers
Armada

by Bryce Walker
and the Editors of Time-Life Books

TIME ®
LIFE

This edition published in 2004
by the Caxton Publishing Group
20 Bloomsbury Street, London WC1B 3JH
Under license from Time-Life Books BV.

Cover Design: Open Door Limited, Rutland UK

The Seafarers
Editorial Staff for *Armada*:
Editor: Anne Horan
Designer: Herbert H. Quarmby
Chief Researcher: W. Mark Hamilton
Picture Editor: Marion F. Briggs
Staff Writers: Kathleen M. Burke, Bobbie Conlan,
Stuart Gannes, Lydia Preston, Mark M. Steele
Researchers: Mindy A. Daniels, Therese Daubner,
Carol A. Enquist, Roxie France, Adrienne George,
Philip Brandt George, Sheila M. Green, Ann Dusel Kuhns,
Anne Muñoz-Furlong
Art Assistant: Michelle René Clay
Editorial Assistant: Ellen Keir

Special Contributors
Richard M. Seamon (essays); Martha Reichard George,
Barbara Hicks (research)

Correspondents: Elisabeth Kraemer (Bonn); Margot
Hapgood, Dorothy Bacon, Lesley Coleman (London); Susan
Jonas, Lucy T. Voulgaris (New York); Maria Vincenza Aloisi,
Josephine du Brusle (Paris); Ann Natanson (Rome).
Valuable assistance was also provided by Wibo van de Linde,
Jenny Hovinga (Amsterdam); Carolyn Montserrat
(Barcelona); Helga Kohl, Martha Mader (Bonn);
Enid Farmer (Boston); Brigid Grauman (Brussels);
Martha de la Cal, Peter Collis (Lisbon); Judy Aspinall, Karin
B. Pearce (London); Jane Walker, Trini Bandres (Madrid);
John Dunn (Melbourne); Carolyn T. Chubet, Miriam Hsia,
Christina Lieberman (New York); Mimi Murphy (Rome);
Janet Zich (San Francisco); Peter Allen (Sydney); Traudl
Lessing (Vienna).

The Author:

BRYCE WALKER, a freelance writer, devoted a year to
researching *Armada*, perusing such vital documents as state
papers signed by the very hand of Queen Elizabeth I. An
aficionado of the sea and its lore ever since he first sailed
in a North Haven dinghy at the age of 10, he has often
managed to combine that love with his work.

The Consultants:

JOHN HORRACE PARRY, Gardiner professor of Oceanic
History and Affairs at Harvard University, is the author of
numerous historical studies, including *The Spanish Seaborne
Empire*.

LOUIS B. WRIGHT is former director of the Folger
Shakespeare Library in Washington, D.C., and the author of
several books on Elizabethan England.

ELAINE W. FOWLER has produced and written numerous
educational films and film-strips, including *"The Spanish
Armada; God's Winds and Broadside Tactics"*.

JOHN FRANCIS GUILMARTIN JR. is a lieutenant colonel
in the United States Air Force and a specialist in the history
of arms. He is editor of the *Air University Review* and the
author of *Gunpowder and Galleys: Changing Technology and
Mediterranean Warfare of Sea in the 16th Century*.

JOSÉ MARÍA MARTÍNEZ-HIDALGO Y TERÁN
is a historian specialising in the achitecture of ships from the
time of Columbus to the end of the 18th Century. He is the
author of the eight-volume *General Encyclopedia of the Sea* and
director of the Reales Atarazanas Maritime Museum in
Barcelona.

WILLIAM AVERY BAKER is a naval architect and engineer.
He was formerly curator of the Hart Nautical Museum at the
Massachusetts Institute of Technology.

Title: The Seafarers, Armada
ISBN: 1 84447 111 X

Contents

Chapter 1

The course toward war

A mighty fleet—one of several armadas the Spanish Empire hurled against foes of the Catholic faith—assaults the Islamic stronghold of Tunis in 1535.

O n a fine June afternoon in 1585, the merchant ship *Primrose*, out of London at 150 tons, lay anchored in the Bay of Biscay off the town of Portugalete, Spain. For the past two days the *Primrose's* crewmen had been unloading a cargo of grain, shifting sacks into a lighter and ferrying them over the sandbar at the harbor entrance to the docking area within. The *Primrose* had discharged more than 20 tons so far. Two other London grain ships lay inside the Portugalete sandbar. Still more were taking off cargoes at other ports in northern Spain—at the nearby city of Bilbao to the east, at Santander to the west, at Corunna beyond.

English ships did not regularly put in at Spanish seaports in 1585. It was a time of bitter, on-again, off-again political squabbles, and in recent months trade between the two countries had all but ceased. But this was an emergency. Spain's wheat crop had failed, and the *Primrose* and her sisters had come by special agreement between the Spanish King and the English Queen to bring relief. As a proof of good faith, the King had issued a guarantee of safe passage to the English ships and crews.

Sometime in midafternoon, a pinnace from the harbor drew up to the *Primrose*; aboard were seven men dressed as merchants and offering baskets of fresh cherries. The *Primrose's* master, Thomas Foster, welcomed them aboard. He laid out what he could in the way of good English cheer: salt beef, ship's biscuit and beer. The Spaniards tucked in with apparent gusto, and made general conversation about ships, cargoes and prices. One of them tried to bargain for the *Primrose's* heavy guns—cannon and culverins of bronze and cast iron carried as defense against pirates. But the first drafts of beer had scarcely been emptied when four of the guests rose from the table and hurried back to town.

Affable as the visitors seemed, something about them touched a suspicious node in Foster's brain. Every Thames bargeman knew of English ships that had been detained in Spanish ports, and of seamen who had disappeared into a Spanish galley or an Inquisition dungeon. Royal guarantee or no, Foster signaled his men to watch out for trouble.

It was well he did. At about 6 o'clock in the evening that June 5th the Spaniards returned in force. They came in two boats—the pinnace with 24 men, trailed by a second vessel carrying perhaps several dozen others. The pinnace pulled alongside and discharged a party of officials. The leader strode up to Foster, who was standing by the mainmast. Foster reacted without hesitation, ordering the rest of the Spaniards to stay in their boats.

They ignored him, swarming up the sides of the *Primrose* and over her decks, brandishing swords and daggers. One man beat a military tattoo on a large drum. Another thrust a dagger at Foster's throat.

"Yield yourself, for you are the King's prisoner!" cried the knife-wielding Spaniard.

"We are betrayed!" yelled Foster, not inclined to yield to anyone.

Neither was any other English seaman. The crewmen had already mustered in the hold and had armed themselves with a grab bag of weaponry: daggers, lances, cudgels, javelins and small-caliber muskets. Most of the men now charged on deck, falling upon the attackers "in such bold and manly sort," wrote a contemporary English scribe, "that they dismayed at every stroke two or three Spaniards." A few men with muskets remained below, and they started shooting up through the hatch gratings. The fire from below caught the Spaniards by surprise; they had routinely stuffed wads of paper into their doublets, but had no protection below the belt. As bullets whizzed menacingly underfoot, the Spaniards suddenly lost their nerve. "Hold your fire!" one cried. "Never," returned Foster, "for so great is the courage of my men that they will slay you, and me too, if need be."

The skirmish lasted only a few minutes, but it sent the Spaniards into full retreat. "Now did their blood runne about the ship in great quantitie," wrote the chronicler, "some of them being shot in between the legges, the bullets issuing foorth at their breasts, some cut in the head, some thrust into the bodie, and many of them very sore wounded. They came not so fast in on the one side, but now they tumbled as fast over boord, with their weapons in their handes."

A fair number jumped to the safety of their boats and headed back to shore. Others splashed into the water and drowned. "It was a great pitie to behold," declared the chronicler, "how the Spanyards lay swimming in the sea, and were not able to save their lives." Four men managed to grab cables dangling from the Primrose's bulwarks; Foster had them hauled aboard as prisoners. He did not pause to tote up the score. He weighed anchor, bent on sail and sped out to sea.

The Primrose's casualties proved to be slight: six wounded, one dead. The men ashore with the grain lighter were now presumably captives, and some cargo had been lost. The Primrose was lucky; of the entire London grain fleet, she is the only vessel known to have escaped. Every other English ship that had been in a Spanish port that first week in June was seized, had her cargo impounded and her crew held in detention.

In escaping, the Primrose came away with some intelligence of singular value. Among the Spaniards she had fished out of the bay was the leader of the assault, who turned out to be acting governor of Biscay province. Asked why he had tried to impound the ship, the official called for his leggings, which were hanging up to dry. From a pocket he took a soggy parchment. It was a commission ordering the take-over.

Its significance was unmistakable. Only one man in Europe could have given such an order—Philip II, His Catholic Majesty the King of Spain, the most powerful monarch in Christendom, and the man who had invited the grain ships in the first place.

The Primrose dropped anchor in the Thames on June 18, just 13 days after her sudden departure from Spain. Notice went immediately to Sir Francis Walsingham, Queen Elizabeth's Principal Secretary and head of her intelligence service. Walsingham called a session of the Privy Council. The four prisoners were hustled off to the Tower of London for questioning, and their answers were forwarded to the council the same day. Beyond the indignity of the impounded grain ships, the council addressed a second issue, far more worrisome. In his commission, King Philip had carefully spelled out his reasons for seizing the ships. He needed them, he wrote, for a massive armada now being readied at Lisbon and Seville, along with soldiers, provisions and armaments.

No one in England knew what such a fleet would be used for. A drive against the Muslims, who sporadically nipped at the eastern fringes of the Spaniards' holdings in Europe? Not likely; the Muslims had been quiet of late. An escort convoy for the annual West Indies treasure shipment? Maybe. An infusion of strength for the Spanish armies fighting rebels in the Netherlands? Perhaps. But there was another possibility, closer to home and far more sinister. To many Englishmen a Spanish armada meant just one thing: a coming invasion of England herself.

England had lived under threat of seaborne attack for as long as anyone could remember. Back in the time of Elizabeth's father, Henry VIII, hostile flotillas from France had twice massed in the Dover Strait—and one had advanced as far as the Isle of Wight before being stopped by Henry's ships. Spain and England had been allies then, but over the years the alliance had begun to break apart. The first hairline cracks began appearing in the 1550s, almost as soon as Philip and Elizabeth came to their respective thrones—though neither monarch wanted trouble. The cracks widened, by jerks and starts. Incidents seemed to erupt spontaneously at opposite sides of the globe, under the impact of mystifying and powerful forces that even the most accomplished of monarchs could not have held back.

When Philip acceded to the crown in 1556, he was a pious and dutiful youth of 28, with more titles to his name than any other monarch in Europe. No one had ever inherited such an array of kingdoms, duchies, counties and principalities. He was King of Spain, Sicily and Naples, of Mexico and Peru, of the Isles and Continents of the Ocean; he was Archduke of Austria, Duke of Burgundy, of Brabant and of Milan, Count of Hapsburg and of Flanders—and so on, like entries in a gazetteer.

Philip bore the weight of these possessions with a devout, if reluctant, will. "Being a king is nothing but a kind of slavery that carries a crown," he once wrote. He saw his kingship as a slavery ordained by God, however, and applied himself with a dedication both stubborn and priestly. Cautious and reticent, clad in clerical black, he would plod through stacks of documents—the reports of governors and ambassadors and viceroys, of customs and treasury officials, the accounts of his mines, his dockyards, his royal household. In a quick, spidery hand he would fill the margins with comments, some shrewd and statesmanlike, some trivial corrections of grammar and spelling. And Philip would deliberate and ponder, and apply God's will as he saw it to his far-flung realm.

God's will toward England, in Philip's view, called for resolute benevolence. In 1554, as a young Prince, he was wed to the island's then reigning Queen, Mary I. The marriage was strictly political, arranged to promote Anglo-Spanish friendship. As Mary's consort, Philip tried doggedly to win over his adopted subjects—without much success. The most notable feature of Mary's reign was her relentless persecution of English Protestants; on one occasion she issued a royal order to immolate some 300 Protestant ecclesiastics on a London hilltop. Philip, Catholic and foreign, had caught much of the blame. He must have felt a fine sense of relief as he headed back home, in 1556, to ascend the Spanish throne on the abdication of his father. However that may be, at Mary's death two years later he offered to marry her half-sister and heir, Eliza-

With her husband, King Philip II of Spain, at her side and two little dogs at her feet, Queen Mary occupies the throne in a medieval English castle. The marriage was unpopular in Protestant England; at the wedding supper the Queen's minions showed their disapproval by serving Philip's meal on a plate of mere silver while Mary supped off one of gold.

beth, in the dutiful thought that Spain and England must stick together.

Elizabeth, who came to the throne in November 1558, was a tall, pale and determined girl of 25, with a high, Tudor brow and hair the color of fox fur. She found the realm a shambles. The treasury was empty, prices were soaring, the army and navy were in decline, a war was rumbling on with France, unrest troubled Scotland and Ireland. "If God start not forth to the helm," lamented a contemporary, "we be at the point of greatest misery that can happen to any people, which is to become thrall of a foreign nation." The clerk need not have worried; no ruler ever held a keener sense of independence than Elizabeth did. She flirted with Philip's offer, then discarded it, as she would a good many others.

Catholics all over Europe, and many in England, were displeased by Elizabeth's accession. They saw her as a heretic, the bastard daughter of Henry VIII and usurper of the English crown. The country's rightful ruler, they believed, was Elizabeth's cousin, the devoutly Catholic Mary Stuart, Queen of Scots. But the new Queen took the helm with a masterly assurance that astonished everyone. "Although I may not be a lion," she told one foreign diplomat, "I am a lion's cub, and I have a lion's heart." She proceeded to end the war with France, to rebuild the navy, to restore the treasury, to reestablish the Church of England, and to woo her people with such style and dedication that she would become the best-loved monarch England ever had. "There was never so wise a woman born," declared a member of her Privy Council, and most of her subjects agreed.

The last thing Elizabeth wanted, as she put her realm in order, was trouble from overseas—particularly from a nation as powerful as Spain. But trouble came, and there seemed to be no stopping it. Partly it was brought on by Elizabeth's own merchant seamen, tough Protestant mariners from Devon, Cornwall and Kent, who were determined to trade wherever they chose, without interference. Some of them ventured west across the Atlantic to the fabulously rich West Indies, where, by papal decree, the right to trade belonged exclusively to Philip of Spain. Others turned pirate; by hitting anywhere on the high seas at Catholic ships, particularly Spanish ones, they could get rich and serve God too. During such incursions, Elizabeth's mariners occasionally ran afoul of the Spanish Inquisition; in 1562, her chief secretary noted, 26 English seamen draped in the hooded yellow robes of heretics were burned at the stake in an auto-da-fé. Elizabeth appeared to pay no heed; she had never overtly endorsed her seamen's marauding, so she was not obligated to avenge them when they got caught. All the same, the incidents rankled.

At home, trouble took the form of agents and missionaries sent out from Rome, under a succession of popes, to unseat Elizabeth and win back England to the Church. And across the Channel, on England's front doorstep, was the most dangerous trouble spot of all: the Netherlands, where in 1566 the Protestant populace rose in revolt against Spanish rule. At the first sign of insurrection, Philip acted. He sent one of his most prominent nobles, Don Fernando Alvarez de Toledo, the Duke of Alba, with 10,300 troops to quash the revolt. This greatly alarmed the English. Here was Europe's best general, with Europe's most powerful army, poised only 40-odd miles from the Dover cliffs. Nothing else made Elizabeth or her advisers quite so nervous.

An elaborate, gilded lock and the royal crest bearing the Latin inscription "Philippus II" adorn this ornate two-and-a-half-foot-long dispatch case. During the 19 months he resided in England while married to Mary, Philip used such cases for filing the correspondence he maintained with his own government.

The first break between Spain and England came in 1568 as the result of two chance events, one in the West Indies, one in the English Channel.

Alba's troops had been on campaign for about six months. To pay them, Philip floated a loan of 450,000 ducats with a banking house in Genoa. The sum, in silver bars, was sent in a group of vessels traveling in convoy but unarmed. This was not a wise move. The sea route from Genoa to Flanders passed through the English Channel, which swarmed with French and Dutch privateers.

Since England and Spain were still, nominally, allies, the ships sought protection from the pirates in various ports along England's southern coast: Falmouth, Plymouth, Southampton. Elizabeth herself agreed to ensure their safety. A plan was worked out with the Spanish Ambassador, Guerau de Spes, to forward the silver overland to an unspecified port in Kent. From there it could be whisked across the Channel to Flanders before the privateers could bend on sail to catch up with it. In early December, Elizabeth gave Spes a safe-conduct order to that effect.

Just then a startling report came in from the New World. A party of English traders had been set upon by Spanish soldiers and killed to the last man. The news was particularly inflammatory in that Queen Elizabeth herself was a shareholder in the trading expedition. She had supplied two ships and had given a royal charter to the leader, John Hawkins of Plymouth. She would have to retaliate. What better riposte than to hold up Alba's silver shipment?

This Elizabeth joyfully did. Her order sped to Southampton countermanding the safe passage. Southampton's governor, acting quickly, told the captain of a Spanish ship that had sought refuge there that his cargo was in grave and immediate danger, that privateers outside the harbor would swoop in and seize it, and that it had better be put ashore at once. The treasure was then packed off, 59 caskets of silver bullion, to the Tower of London. Similar orders went to Plymouth and Falmouth. There, too, Spanish silver was unloaded and sent to London.

Local seamen, generally anti-Spanish on principle, were delighted. "Great pity it were such a rich booty should escape her Grace," declared an English vice admiral.

Ambassador Spes was outraged. He drafted an urgent dispatch to Alba, saying, in effect: Elizabeth has hijacked your payroll—do something. On December 29, Alba impounded all English property in the Netherlands. That was a serious mistake. Elizabeth struck back by seizing all Spanish goods in England, gaining far more than the value of English goods taken abroad. And she also had the silver. There was enough to maintain her navy for months, with some left over to send as discreet aid to Alba's foes, the Dutch rebels. Philip angrily responded by imposing an embargo on English trade in all Spanish ports.

Evidence of what had really happened in the Caribbean arrived about a month later. On January 25 a seaworn, bullet-scarred vessel creaked into harbor in Cornwall with 15 half-starved crewmen and a tale that would further unravel the ties between Spain and England. She was the 31-year-old *Minion*, one of the two royal ships that had sailed with John Hawkins to the Indies.

Hawkins stumbled ashore and explained that he had been ambushed

Two incidents of persecution—
the hanging and dismembering of Catholic
churchmen in 1530 during King Henry
VIII's reign (below) and the burning of the
Protestant Archbishop of Canterbury
at Queen Mary's behest in 1556 (right)—
exemplify the violent religious stresses
afflicting England as monarchs of different
faiths came to power. Throughout the
16th Century, affairs of church and state
were so intertwined that heresy and
treason were thought to be synonymous.

by a Spanish fleet while lying at anchor in San Juan de Ulúa on the Mexican coast. The English had put up a heroic fight, against huge odds, but had finally been routed. The Queen's second ship, the *Jesus of Lubeck*, had been sunk. Three of Hawkins' own ships were missing. Of 408 men and boys on the expedition, most were dead or captive.

It made no difference to Elizabeth and her counselors that Hawkins had broken Philip's embargo on trade in the West Indies and was poaching in Spanish waters. Nor did it matter that his principal cargo had been African slaves—a monopoly Philip reserved for himself. What mattered was this: The incident at San Juan de Ulúa was the first exchange of gunfire between ships flying the castles of Philip and ships carrying the lions and lilies of Elizabeth. It was a violent prelude to the years ahead.

John Hawkins was an unlikely man to initiate the new phase of international relations; nothing marked him as a troublemaker. Tall, tough-willed, with a long, bony, poker face and an engaging courtesy, he seemed more like an alderman or a judge than a roguish sea dog. "I have always hated folly," he once said—a sentiment that was only proper in a scion of Plymouth's leading merchant family. As a young sea trader in the Canary Islands, Hawkins had paid scrupulous attention to local law and custom. When among Spaniards, he would speak of Philip as "the king, my master." Yet because he so profoundly believed that England had a God-given right to trade, he dared to challenge the King's monopoly in the Caribbean. He seemed to be purposely testing Philip's right to bar English seamen from the riches of the New World. To Philip, such behavior was insufferable. In the margins of dispatches the King would scribble *Ojo!*—"Watch out!"—beside every mention of the Englishman's name. Strong protests were lodged with the English government.

Whatever the international consequences of Hawkins' poaching, it had left him considerably out of pocket—by £28,000, according to his own estimate. What is more, Hawkins had been forced to leave a number of comrades behind in Mexico. His last words to them had been a promise: He would return to rescue them.

Another expedition would be needed, and Hawkins began fitting out 10 warships. He would sail to the Caribbean, free his old shipmates, and on the way back capture Philip's West Indies treasure fleet, worth an estimated six million pounds. But Elizabeth, anxious to avoid further hostility, would not let him leave.

With force ruled out, Hawkins resolved on a wily approach to the Spanish Ambassador, Guerau de Spes. Perhaps the Spaniards would be receptive to a deal.

Hawkins was a man of considerable persuasiveness, with a talent for the bold bluff. Queen Elizabeth, he told Spes, was a difficult patron and he was growing restless in her service. For the return of his friends, perhaps there was some small service he could perform for King Philip?

Perhaps so, allowed Spes, who was working on a deal of his own. The Ambassador's scheme reached to the very highest centers of power in Europe, and would further destroy the crumbling accord between England and Spain. It involved nothing less than the invasion of England, the overthrow of Queen Elizabeth, and the crowning of her Catholic

Sir John Hawkins, one of the 16th Century's most daring naval adventurers, wears the finery of an Elizabethan gentleman in this contemporary portrait. An outspoken champion of England's right to trade anywhere in the world, he practiced what he preached—and inflamed Spanish wrath by selling African slaves and English goods in the West Indies, where Spain claimed a monopoly.

cousin Mary Stuart. For various reasons of local politics, Mary had fled Scotland in 1568 and was now in England under virtual house arrest.

Spes's plot, hatched with the help of an Italian banker named Roberto Ridolfi, called for England's Catholic nobles, led by the powerful Duke of Norfolk, to stage a revolt. In support, 8,000 Spanish soldiers under the Duke of Alba would cross the Channel and land at Portsmouth and Harwich. Elizabeth would be deposed and Mary crowned Queen. Mary was enthusiastic, Norfolk was persuaded, and Ridolfi traveled to Flanders to enlist Alba. The Duke thought the plan ridiculous and pronounced Ridolfi "a great babbler." But he too was finally hectored into it. There was, however, a major problem: how to bring troops from the Netherlands while Dutch and English ships patrolled the Channel.

The answer lay with Hawkins, who neatly inserted himself into the plot. The Channel's western approaches were guarded by a squadron of armed private merchantmen operating out of the Devon ports, with Hawkins in general command. All the Englishman needed to do was to lead the squadron east and rendezvous with Alba. Thus covered, the Spanish troops could ferry over unmolested. Did the Englishman agree? His poker face showing nothing, Hawkins said yes.

Spes reported back to Ridolfi, and Ridolfi bounced off to Madrid to lay the plan before Philip. The King listened, but with reservations. He was a cautious man, known by all as the Prudent Prince. Ridolfi's plot might well entangle him in an all-out war, and Philip hated war, as one partisan said, "as a burned child hates the fire." And what about this wretched Hawkins? Could he be trusted?

After much pressing by Ridolfi, Philip agreed to sponsor the plan. He wrote out a pardon for all Hawkins' insults in the Caribbean, granted him a patent of nobility, and promised 40,000 ducats for the upkeep of Hawkins' ships. And he released Hawkins' shipmates.

In England, there was no doubt where Hawkins' loyalty lay. He had reported every wrinkle of the convoluted scheme to William Cecil, Lord Burghley, Elizabeth's sagacious chief minister. "Great titles and honors from the King!" Hawkins scoffed; "God deliver me!" Burghley already had his own line on the plotters, and with Hawkins' corroborating testimony he could now round them up. Spes was handed his papers, and diplomatic ties were thus severed. Spain's first grand invasion scheme had been strangled at birth.

The argument between the two countries droned on in fits and starts, like a family feud, the stormy spells followed by brief periods of almost sunny reconciliation. In time, ambassadors were again exchanged. The European trade embargo, in effect since Alba lost his payroll, was lifted—although Elizabeth kept the silver as compensation for the losses at San Juan de Ulúa. By 1573 English merchants were again peddling their linens and woolens in Iberian ports. Philip recalled Alba from the Netherlands, where his harsh policies were doing nothing to hold that rebellious land in check for the Spanish Empire. But the storm clouds continued massing, and Philip and Elizabeth were no more able to hold them back than they could have held back the weather.

The most dangerous pressure point was still the Netherlands, where the Protestant revolt continued to sputter and flame. Squads of privateers, forbidden to prey on Spanish ships in English waters during one of the spells when England and Spain were on good terms, had seized the ports of Brielle and Flushing. There, under the name of Sea Beggars, they began operating as an independent Protestant navy against the Spaniards (pages 30-37). A number of English cavaliers, out to win their spurs in the field, crossed the Channel to fight in the rebel army. Officially Elizabeth gave no endorsement to these activities, but whenever the Spaniards seemed close to victory she felt compelled to help the Protestants by sending them secret shipments of arms and money.

In the New World, English seamen began raiding Spanish ships and settlements. Hawkins' young cousin Francis Drake, who also had escaped from San Juan de Ulúa, sped back to the Caribbean to take reprisals. By 1573 he had looted the colonies of more than £40,000. Another Plymouth captain, Gilbert Horseley, sailed west in 1574 in an 18-ton cockleshell of a boat, with only 13 little guns, and sailed home again with at least £2,000 in captured treasure. There were dozens more. Some were caught by the Spaniards and imprisoned as pirates or relieved of their heads. But enough got through to cause the Spanish King considerable dismay.

England itself lived in a state of chronic anxiety. An undercover army of missionary priests from Rome preached dissent in parishes across the land, throwing salt in old religious wounds. There were new plots against Elizabeth and new schemes to assault the realm. "The state of Christendom dependeth upon the stout assailing of England," said one agitator. In 1579 foreign invaders landed on the west coast of Ireland, part of Elizabeth's territory and disturbingly close to home. Potentially, the attempt was explosive; in execution it was almost laughable.

The force that disembarked on July 17 near Dingle Bay, in southwestern Ireland, was scarcely an army. It was a ragtag company of Spanish, English and Italian volunteers who had sailed in three ships from northern Spain. Its commander was a renegade Irishman named James Fitzmaurice, who was whipped on by an agent of the Pope. Despite the doubtful strength of the invaders, they gave London a fright. Elizabeth mobilized a 3,000-man army and sent a squadron of ships to the Irish coast. The overmatched intruders lay low, and after three months of uneventful patrolling, the English squadron was disbanded.

Meanwhile, Fitzmaurice left his company awaiting reinforcements at Smerwick, north of Dingle Bay, and went off in search of help from Irish leaders—only to be killed in an inland skirmish when he tried to commandeer some farmers' horses. Late the next summer, papal reinforcements for the invasion effort finally arrived. Eight ships out of Santander in northern Spain, flying the Vatican flag from their maintops and the banner of Spain from their foretops, sailed into Smerwick harbor. Some 700 or 800 volunteers put ashore. They lugged with them more than 100 artillery pieces and an arsenal of 2,000 muskets and harquebuses. The landing proceeded without a hitch—not surprisingly, since the admiral in charge was one of Spain's ablest and proudest seamen, Don Juan Martínez de Recalde, a fiery Basque nobleman from Bilbao who normally commanded the elite convoy squadron attached to the West Indies treasure fleet. He was now acting privately to deliver a blow against heresy. The landing accomplished, Recalde spent a few weeks surveying the largely uncharted Irish coast before heading back home. The volunteers he left behind set up their cannon in a low earthwork fortification on the water's edge and sat tight.

London soon learned of the Recalde landing. Sir William Wynter, Surveyor of Ships on the Navy Board and a veteran fighter, quickly fitted out a fleet and on September 25 set out for Ireland with nine warships, plus pinnaces and victualers.

Wynter sailed in the fast, newly built 500-ton *Revenge*, the crack warship in Elizabeth's fleet. Behind him came two slightly smaller ships, the *Swiftsure* and the *Aid*, followed by various vessels, mostly in the 100- to 300-ton range. One, the tiny *Achates*, was captained by his son William Wynter II. Because the ships were scattered in a storm, the *Swiftsure* reached Smerwick first, sweeping into the harbor on November 7 and taking immediate charge. She drove a heavily laden Spanish supply ship onto the rocks and sent the crew scurrying for protection in the fort. Then she dropped anchor to await Wynter and the others.

Wynter pulled in two days later with the rest of the squadron. His first step was to bombard the fort, which—conveniently for the attackers—protruded conspicuously into the harbor like a beached ship. The three large vessels—the *Revenge*, the *Swiftsure* and the *Aid*—were too deep-drafted to approach the shore. But Wynter devised tactics that were ingenious and devastating. He anchored the three big warships in mid-harbor; from there they lobbed shot at the fort with long-range culverins that were mounted high in their bows. The smaller ships—the *Merlin*, the *Tiger* and the *Achates*—circled close to shore, single file, in front of the fort. As each vessel neared land it fired its bow piece. Wheeling around, it delivered a broadside, followed by a parting shot from its stern guns on the way out. Then the next ship moved through the sequence: bow shot, broadside, stern shot. The barrage continued without pause, since each vessel reloaded during the return leg.

A circle of ships moving single file past a target: Wynter's tactic marked a breakthrough in English naval practice. Most commanders attacked in a line-abreast formation, their ships ranged side by side like a wave of charging cavalry. But the English would fall into this new line-ahead formation frequently in the years to come, using it against the Spanish Armada when it arrived. Eventually line ahead would become standard naval tactics. Right now, Wynter's bombardment did considerable damage to the seaward side of the Smerwick fort.

The *coup de grâce* was administered the next day by the English army. Coincidentally with Wynter's arrival by sea, Lord Grey de Wilton, Lord Deputy of Ireland, had marched into Smerwick from Dingle with 800 men. He set up a battery of eight culverins on the fort's landward side and loosed a hail of great shot, blasting the fort's own artillery into silence. A defender leaped up on the battlements waving a white sheet.

There followed one of the bloodier moments of Elizabeth's turbulent reign. The defenders agreed to lay down their arms provided their lives were spared. Grey made no promises, but simply accepted the surrender. He held the officers for ransom, a standard practice of the day. He had a crueler fate in store for the troops; his soldiers slaughtered every last

man of them, driving a sword or a pike through each of the 507 Spaniards and Italians, and torturing and hanging 17 Irishmen and Englishmen remaining from Fitzmaurice's disorganized venture. Grey's troops also killed several pregnant women and a priest. The defenders held no commission from a reigning prince, Grey pointed out. They were traitors and pirates, nothing more.

News of the Smerwick massacre was received in Europe with remarkable equanimity. Catholics seemed more indignant that the volunteers had surrendered than that they had been killed. "So little inflamed with military ardor" were they, complained a Vatican official, "that they were accustomed to use their swords as spits, and their helmets as pots when cooking their meat." Philip had a new and outspoken ambassador in London, Bernardino de Mendoza, who called the volunteers and their action plain stupid. "Impossible to have found a worse place to build a fort," he wrote the King; "it had no natural capabilities for defense, and did not even possess the neighborhood wood for fuel."

Philip took three months to comment. Finally, he allowed that he was grieved by the death of the soldiers, but more particularly by their cowardly behavior. The venture was not his concern, however. It had been arranged by the Pope, not by him. Philip had been happy to let the volunteers use his ports, even to lend them money. But he had given them no patent to make war with Elizabeth.

That was true enough; the Spanish King was engaged in an enterprise of far greater moment on another front, one that would double the size of his global might and throw Europe's balance of power on its beam ends. He was in the process of annexing the kingdom of Portugal. Philip the Prudent liked nothing so much as a sure thing, and Portugal was sure.

In 1580 the Portuguese King had died without issue. Philip was a close cousin. Now that the redoubtable Duke of Alba was no longer preoccupied in the Netherlands, Philip sent him on a triumphal parade through the Tagus River valley toward Lisbon to secure Portugal's throne. Spain's leading admiral, Don Alvaro de Bazán, the Marquis of Santa Cruz, sailed up the mouth of the Tagus into Lisbon harbor to support Alba's land operation. By late August 1580, the Spanish flag was rippling from the battlements of Lisbon's royal palace. Philip had already eased the take-over of Portugal with payments of land and titles to the nobility. He later boasted, "I inherited it, I purchased it, I conquered it."

Philip's masterful triple stroke sent flurries of alarm through the rest of Europe. Not only did the Spanish King now control the entire Iberian Peninsula, but he had gained title to Portugal's network of priceless colonial properties. To the riches he already possessed in the West Indies, he added the silks and spices of the East Indies, the gold and slaves of west Africa, the wood of Brazil and Madeira, and the provisioning base of the Cape Verde Islands. Philip also acquired something else, equally significant: a true oceangoing navy.

Most of Spain's sea power before now had taken the form of oared galleys. Although these were superb weapons in enclosed waters such as the Mediterranean, they were too flimsy and short-range to be very useful on the high seas. Galleys, many of them Spanish, had won Christian Europe's resounding victory nine years earlier over the Turks at

Lepanto, so far the century's greatest naval battle. But with the exception of the West Indies convoy squadron, Philip owned no fighting sail for work on the ocean. When he needed an Atlantic fleet he had to commandeer armed merchantmen in Spanish ports, or hire warships from other countries—often from England.

Portugal had ships and sailors and the strongest seafaring tradition in Europe. Portuguese mariners had been the first to explore the far reaches of the Atlantic, the first to battle the seas around the Cape of Good Hope, the first to ride the monsoons in the Indian Ocean. Portuguese warships were renowned for size, sturdiness and sea-keeping ability. In Lisbon harbor, Santa Cruz had captured intact 11 fine oceangoing Portuguese galleons. These mighty square-riggers, ships ranging in size from 700 to 1,000 tons, would become the elite first line of Philip's navy.

Philip soon called the new force into action, sending it to the one key sector of Portuguese territory that remained untaken—the Azores, a cluster of nine islands strategically located in mid-Atlantic, along the

Warships and commercial vessels crowd the bustling port of Lisbon in this 16th Century woodcut by the Dutch engraver Theodore de Bry. In seizing Portugal in 1580, Philip II gained possession of a vast colonial empire that, when added to his own, accorded him suzerainty over more than half the habitable surface of the earth.

trade route from the West Indies. The Azores were holding out for a rival claimant to the throne, the Portuguese-born Don Antonio, Prior of Crato, who was an illegitimate cousin of the late King's predecessor. Don Antonio's agents had set up headquarters on Terceira, the second largest of the islands, and he himself was drumming up support in the major courts of Europe.

Don Antonio's plan was to raise an army of mercenaries and a fleet to carry them to Terceira. From there he would launch the reconquest of his homeland. The pretender applied first to England, presenting Elizabeth with an enormous diamond ring from Portugal's collection of crown jewels. The Queen, distressed by Philip's sudden gain in power and prestige, listened with apparent enthusiasm. Keeping the ring as surety, she lent Don Antonio money to build ships and to marshal troops. But the pretender's hopes of further English assistance soon bogged down in Elizabeth's esoteric games of international politics. Don Antonio turned in disgust to France.

Here he struck gold. The French King, while avowing that officially he could do nothing to help, subtly let it be known that his mother also had a claim to the Portuguese throne, and that she too was alarmed by Philip's new glory. Arrangements were made—in deep secrecy, of course—to lend Don Antonio the services of Filippo Strozzi, a Florentine nobleman and favorite cousin of the Queen Mother. Strozzi, who resided in France, mustered a force of 6,000 soldiers, along with a great fleet of some 60 ships. On June 16, 1582, this grand flotilla left the port of Belle-Ile, off the Brittany coast, and headed west for the Azores.

Philip's corps of international spies had followed every twist and jog of Don Antonio's progress, and had reported the details to Madrid. A Spanish fleet to intercept Strozzi, 36 ships strong, was already in the final stages of hurried mobilization at Lisbon. To command it, Philip turned once again to Don Alvaro de Bazán, the Marquis of Santa Cruz, his premier admiral, whose deft thrust up the Tagus had secured the 11 Portuguese galleons.

Santa Cruz had survived more campaigns and won more distinction than any other seaman in Spain. Now a grizzled 56, he held a reputation as a daring and skilled tactician. As commander of the rear guard of galleys at Lepanto, he had dashed into a breach in the front line, thereby heading off a jab by the Turkish vice admiral and establishing himself as a national hero. Galley tactics were the marquis's specialty, in fact. Now, with a flotilla of galleons and greatships—merchantmen converted to war duty—he was about to test his genius in an unprecedented type of naval combat. Never before had sailing ships of such mammoth size and mighty armament fought on the open sea. The topsides of both fleets were studded with heavy guns, the bellies of both were weighted with powder and shot, water kegs and provisions. The rules for the game they would play had not yet been written.

Santa Cruz hustled out of Lisbon on July 10—later than he should have if he wanted to beat Strozzi to the Azores, though with luck he might still catch up. His fleet presented a formidable array. As flagship he had chosen one of the captured Portuguese galleons, the 48-gun *San Martín*, a 1,000-ton giant. Another Portuguese galleon, the 750-ton

Filippo Strozzi, who commanded the French fleet against the Spaniards in the Azores in 1582, was kin to Florentine nobles and French royalty. As a confidant of Catherine de' Medici —mother of the King of France—he often served as emissary for the Crown.

San Mateo, carried General Lope de Figueroa, in charge of a 250-man force of swordsmen, pikemen and harquebusiers. Then came veteran marine fighter Don Miguel de Oquendo with a squadron of converted merchantmen bristling with cannon and culverins; then more armed merchantmen from Portugal, from the Baltic, from the provinces of Castile and Guipúzcoa; then cargo hulks and victualers, dispatch boats and patrol craft, a hospital ship—36 sail in all. The French force was even larger, but Santa Cruz expected reinforcements shortly; Martínez de Recalde was mobilizing a reserve fleet in Cádiz.

Delays plagued the fleet at the start. This was not the season for Atlantic storms, but the Spaniards managed to find one. Four vessels, including the hospital ship, limped back to Lisbon. Others were blown off course and had to regroup. By the time Santa Cruz dropped anchor at Villafranca on the south coast of the island of São Miguel on July 22, the French had already been in the Azores six days.

The marquis dispatched a patrol under Oquendo to reconnoiter the French fleet. Oquendo headed for Punta Delgada, the island's main harbor 12 miles to the west, and arrived just in time to watch the French standing out to sea. Oquendo counted 56 sail, though he may have missed a few ships in the van.

On this intelligence the marquis summoned his commanders for a

quick conference. Should they wait for the reserve fleet under Recalde,
or should they seek a battle immediately, outnumbered though they
were? With the same headlong appetite for glory that had won at Lepanto, the commanders voted to fight.

Santa Cruz drew his fleet into a tight battle formation, line abreast,
opposite the French. The San Martín rode in the center of the line,
flanked left and right by the next six strongest vessels. It was a classic
configuration—for galleys. The Spaniards would have to wait to see
how it worked with galleons, however, for the ships were now reduced
to helpless immobility by a prosaic event: The wind died. The two fleets
spent the night drifting about outside Punta Delgada.

For the next three days the fleets stalked each other in light westerly
airs south of São Miguel, sparring gingerly on the wings but never clos-
ing in full battle. Periodically, a French detachment would glide down
toward one of the Spanish flanks in an attempt to cut off the outermost
ships. Each time, Santa Cruz was able to turn his fleet to meet them. Each
time, the French would withdraw. The afternoon of the second day saw
the only real action. Near the eastern tip of São Miguel, the French bore
down in force with three full squadrons. Oquendo, commanding the
Spanish rear guard, turned to face them. The San Martín and San Mateo,
downwind at the time, clawed back up to assist. There was a brief,

intense skirmish with heavy cannonading by both sides. A Spanish dispatch boat took heavy damage below the water line and had to be abandoned. The damage ended there. Again the French withdrew.

Nothing could have been more frustrating to a commander of Santa Cruz's caliber than this kind of inconclusive fencing. There was little he could do about it, however, since the French had worked themselves into a key tactical position. Each day the wind had come up from the west, behind the French fleet and into the faces of the Spaniards. This possession of the windward position—the so-called weather gauge—gave the French the advantage in maneuvering. They could swoop down at will on any section of the Spanish line they wished, or they could hold off indefinitely, hoping to pick up laggard vessels one at a time. The Spaniards, caught to leeward, could do nothing but wait. To try attacking upwind with a fleet of cumbersome, square-rigged sailing ships would be like sending a regiment into battle wearing lead boots.

The Spanish repeatedly attempted to gain the weather gauge, but the enemy ships were simply too quick and handy, always managing to slip back upwind. Then on the night of the 24th, Santa Cruz turned his fleet about under cover of darkness and, helped on by a freshening breeze, worked his way to windward undetected. By the following morning he had moved in behind Strozzi's fleet and had the wind at his back.

Santa Cruz drew his ships line abreast and signaled the attack with a single artillery blast followed by a blare of trumpets. More frustration ensued. The Spanish vice admiral, Don Cristobal de Eraso, snapped his mainmast, putting a key frontline ship out of commission. The marquis halted the attack and spun the *San Martín* around to take Eraso in tow. Another day had been wasted.

July 26 dawned flat and breathless. Eighteen miles offshore and two or three miles apart, both fleets drifted, their sails sagging lifelessly from the yards. A little after 8 a.m. the sails began to lift. The wind picked up from the west, and once again the French, who were to the northwest, had the weather gauge. But this time it was different. Around midday, as both fleets reached north past São Miguel, the French were tracking in a long file to the west, the Spaniards paralleling them to the east. Gradually, as though by chance, the 750-ton galleon *San Mateo* began to ease out of line toward the French fleet. Whether the commander, Lope de Figueroa, was acting under orders or whether he was breaking formation on his own, out of sheer, exasperated pugnacity, no one knows. Either way, he was soon moving in splendid, highly vulnerable isolation midway between the two fleets.

Strozzi had been waiting for just such an opportunity. His tactics all along had been to cut off individual ships or squadrons in the hope of overwhelming them by superior numbers. Here was the second most important vessel in the Spanish fleet, presented as a gift. Strozzi bore down with his five strongest sail: his own flagship, his vice admiral's ship, or *almiranta*, and three smaller galleons.

Figueroa braced for the attack. The *San Mateo's* guns, some 30 bronze cannon and culverins ranged in two tiers on either broadside, were charged with shot and primed. Crack musketeers climbed aloft into the crosstrees. The ship's 250 soldiers took stations in the towering castles,

Off Terceira Island in 1583, workmen make repairs on the rigging of a Spanish galleon—one of about a dozen such vessels that were stationed in the Azores to guard against any attempt by the Portuguese to recapture the islands.

fore and aft, poised to repel boarders. The encounter gave promise of being hot and bloody. It was.

Strozzi's flagship struck first, in a blaze of gunfire, swinging in on the port bow and smashing into the *San Mateo*'s bowsprit. Figueroa waited until no more than a yardarm's length separated the two hulls, then loosed his first shuddering broadside. The French almiranta slid up to starboard, and a second Spanish broadside came, delivered point-blank. Great shot pounded in on both sides now, as the two Frenchmen subjected the *San Mateo* to a deadly cross fire. Grappling hooks swung in from port and starboard, snagging rigging and bulwarks and locking the three ships together in a cat's cradle of hawsers. The three smaller galleons, meanwhile, hovered at the *San Mateo*'s quarters, raking her sterncastle.

For two hours the five French vessels blasted the *San Mateo*, riddling her hull with more than 500 cannon rounds, shooting away her masts and rigging, splattering her decks with shrapnel from stone-heaving, mortar-like perriers. Some 20 fires sprang up from incendiary charges of burning pitch. A choking, prickling envelope of smoke folded so thickly over the Spanish ship that her musketeers could hardly see to aim their weapons. So deafening was the thunder of heavy guns that a priest, administering last rites in the relative safety of the hold, dropped dead of a heart attack. Nearly half the company was cut down, dead or wounded, by gunshot or saber gash.

Yet somehow the Spaniards held out. In bitter hand-to-hand combat as the French tried time and again to board, men would fall wounded, pick themselves up and spring back fighting. At one point Figueroa ordered his lieutenants to strike down any Spaniard who tried to carry the fight to the French flagship: The instinct to attack ran so strong that it would have left the *San Mateo* defenseless.

While the *San Mateo* fought its lone, deadly bout with the pick of the enemy, the rest of the Spanish fleet hauled steadily up to help. From its downwind position to the east, the fleet took more than two hours to reach the action. First to arrive was the rear guard of armed merchantmen, commanded by Oquendo. The 350-ton *Juana* pulled up on the far side of the French flagship, nearly twice her size, and unleashed a broadside. Another merchantman attacked the almiranta.

Oquendo himself came up next and delivered the most flamboyantly effective stroke of the day. He rammed his ship full speed between the almiranta and the *San Mateo*, smashing the Frenchman's side and snapping the cables that bound the two combatants together. "He handled his ship like a cavalryman handling his horse," marveled one observer. There was a fierce artillery exchange, one broadside killing 50 men aboard the almiranta. Oquendo heaved grappling lines, stormed the sterncastle and cut down the French flag, replacing it with his own. By now both ships were badly holed and filling with water. Oquendo cut loose and left the Frenchman to sink.

The two fleets had now converged, and the fighting spread into a general melee. Neither side attempted to maintain an orderly battle line. Each captain looked for an opponent, opened fire, then grappled and boarded. It was the bloodiest kind of combat, giving rise to deeds of high valor—and occasional grandstand heroics. One French ensign, his ship overrun, was seen standing in the prow, wrapped in the French flag. He then jumped, carrying the flag into the ocean with him lest it be captured and disgraced. There were also some sorry defections: The French rear guard, for reasons unknown, never joined the battle.

Santa Cruz hunted through the smoke and chaos, aiding where needed, searching for Strozzi's flagship. After the rescuing charge by Oquendo's squadron, Strozzi had cut himself free of the *San Mateo* and was drifting alone. Santa Cruz finally spotted him and approached with two ships. The French vessel was pummeled with great shot until she began to sink. The marquis proceeded to board.

Strozzi was ready to quit in any case. He had been fighting for five hours straight, some 400 of his men were dead, his decks ran with blood, the ocean was gushing into his hold, and he himself was near death from a harquebus wound. He was carried aboard the *San Martín* to surrender, but he never had the chance. He expired before handing over his sword. Santa Cruz had his body thrown into the sea.

The day was now a clear Spanish triumph. The French, at the loss of their flagship, turned and fled. Santa Cruz had delivered a stunning display of Spain's new sea power. Against heavy odds he had sustained only moderate casualties: 224 dead, 553 wounded, only one small dispatch boat lost. He had taken a staggering toll. French casualties were estimated at between 1,200 and 1,500 dead. The French had lost 11 ships: the flagship captured, two large warships burned, four sunk, four others sacked and abandoned to the sea.

Spain's victory was not yet total, however. The Portuguese pretender, for whose benefit the fleets had clashed, was still at large. Don Antonio had traveled to the Azores with the French, but he had put ashore at Terceira before the fight. He was now busy setting up a government-in-exile. If the Spanish men had been fresh and the ships undamaged, Santa Cruz would most certainly have sought him out.

This was not the moment to continue the campaign on land, however. Santa Cruz touched shore only to take on water—and to execute his prisoners. Like the volunteers at Smerwick, they were deemed only pirates and traitors, and—said the marquis—deserved hanging "for the glory of God and the King our master." He then headed back to Lisbon to patch his ships and deliver his wounded to the hospital.

The following summer Santa Cruz sailed out to complete the conquest of the Azores. After his hard-won success off São Miguel, this 1583 campaign seemed almost like a weekend romp. He arrived off Terceira in mid-July with 98 warships and an army of 15,372 men. Within two weeks he had subdued the entire archipelago, hanged Don Antonio's governor (the pretender himself had fled to France, again missing the action), and had set his helm back toward Spain.

Never had a Spanish hero come home to such acclaim. Santa Cruz was lauded by the Cortes, Spain's parliament, in an unprecedented ovation. Philip ordered a *Te Deum* Mass in his honor at the royal monastery at El Escorial, outside Madrid. The marquis was named a grandee of Spain, and given the rarely bestowed title Captain General of the Ocean Sea.

In the euphoria of victory, Santa Cruz made an astonishing assertion to Philip. "Now that we have all Portugal," the admiral wrote, "England is

In a show of strength that sends the Portuguese scurrying into the hills of Terceira Island, Spanish troops march in precise formation—swordsmen on the perimeter, lancers in the center—while boatloads more are rowed ashore.

ours." (In smashing the French at São Miguel, the marquis thought he had bested some freelance English ships as well. Perhaps he had, though the English left no record of it.)

England. Once again that stubborn, cantankerous island, that sorry land of damp weather and dreadful heresy. The topic seemed perpetually to blight Philip's reign. Despite the provocations of the Queen, despite the cries for action from his advisers, from the Pope, from Catholics everywhere in Europe, Philip had done his best to keep the peace. Now here was his best admiral offering to take on the whole English navy—suggesting, in fact, an invasion. Philip had to listen.

At Philip's request, Santa Cruz drew up an invasion plan. He asked for 150 galleons and armed merchantmen, 40 cargo hulks to carry supplies, some 320 dispatch boats and other auxiliaries—a total of 510 sail, not counting 40-odd oar-powered vessels. The fleet he proposed would be the largest armada Europe had ever seen, and it would require 30,000 mariners and would carry 64,000 assault troops. The cost would run well over 3.8 million ducats.

Santa Cruz was asking the impossible, for at least two reasons. Philip's treasury held no such sum. And assembling such a force would strip the harbors of Spain and Portugal of shipping essential to the countries' economic sustenance. Still, the King did not reject the plan out of hand. He studied the figures, weighed the risks, mulled over the probable consequences. Slowly the notion of an assault on England changed from a nagging, improbable whim to a clear option of state policy.

While Philip deliberated, hostilities between England and Spain took on a new intensity. England's privateering raids grew more ambitious, Spanish victories in the Netherlands more frequent and more alarming to Elizabeth. Assassination plots against the Queen came to light with grim regularity. One scheme in 1583, involving some Jesuit priests and an invasion force from France, also implicated the Spanish Ambassador. Again diplomatic ties were cut. The following year, a delegation from Holland arrived at Whitehall with news that the great Dutch leader William of Orange had been shot to death on the stairway of his house at Delft by a paid agent of King Philip.

Such was the climate as the year moved into 1585. The last hopes for peace were guttering; events were moving pell-mell into crisis.

It was at this point, in June 1585, that the grain ship *Primrose* nosed into harbor with her four Spanish prisoners and her tale of attempted brigandage. No wonder the documents she carried took on a terrible urgency and significance. No wonder people thought the armada then gathering would indeed thunder down upon England.

England reacted not with fear but with outrage. The London merchants demanded reprisals for their impounded ships. "Her Majesty will not endure the indignity unrequited," fumed one shipowner, who cried out for "publicke warr" against the Spanish King. Another, noting that the Biscay seamen who served in Philip's summer campaigns spent the winter fishing for cod off Newfoundland, offered to stop the invasion singlehandedly. "Give me five ships," he wrote Elizabeth, "and I will go out and sink them all, and the galleons shall rot in Cadiz harbor for want of hands to sail them."

In a satirical 16th Century painting, Philip II sits astride a cow symbolizing the Netherlands, as his functionary the Duke of Alba milks her, the Duke of Alençon (representing France) pulls her tail, Queen Elizabeth feeds her hay and the Dutch rebel leader William of Orange tries to steady the animal. During the 16th Century, all Europe meddled in the affairs of the Netherlands.

The Queen needed no further persuading. Letters of marque authorizing reprisals against Spanish shipping went out to the aggrieved shipowners. A royal squadron sailed to Newfoundland. Elizabeth's most prominent general, the imperious Earl of Leicester, crossed the Channel to Flushing with an army of 5,000 foot soldiers and 1,000 horses, bringing England's first overt intervention in the Dutch revolt. The nation's most dashing and aggressive seaman, Francis Drake (who had looted an extraordinary £600,000 of Spanish treasure when he sailed around the world a few years earlier), set off with 27 ships and 2,300 troops to burn and pillage Philip's Atlantic and Caribbean islands. But all these were mere forays designed to harass Spain. At the royal dockyards south of London, John Hawkins redoubled his efforts on a project dear to his heart—a massive refurbishing of the Queen's naval forces, to ensure that England would be ready for anything.

The Sea Beggars: pirates with royal backing

BRIEL

William von Lumey, commander of the Beggars when they scored their first major victory (opposite), so hated Spain that he vowed not to cut his hair or fingernails until the rebel cause was won.

On a spring morning in 1566, a group of Dutch noblemen rode into Brussels, capital of the Spanish imperial administration in the Netherlands, and demanded an audience with the Duchess Margaret of Parma, regent for the King of Spain. For a time she listened as the nobles complained bitterly about their subordination to Spanish officialdom, the crushing taxation and Spain's harsh measures against Protestantism. Finally, exasperated beyond endurance by their stridency, she swept from the room in tears. Following close on her heels went an aide, who offered her consolation. "What, Madame," he whispered—none too softly—"afraid of these beggars?"

The remark proved monumentally unwise. When the noblemen met again to assess their plight, one of them burlesqued the gibe, waving aloft a wooden bowl of the kind used by Dutch mendicants. At that point—according to a participant—the entire assemblage sprang to its feet with the fervent cry, "Long live the Beggars!" In a single stroke, the Dutch independence movement was born, complete with a battle cry and a catchy designation for the insurgents themselves.

Nowhere did the Beggars more actively press their cause than at sea. The English Channel already swarmed with pirates who preyed upon merchant shipping without regard to nationality. Now hundreds of Dutchmen, fleeing stepped-up oppression on land, took to the sea and joined the pirates. Prince William of Orange, the leader of the Beggars movement, gave them respectability, issuing letters of marque that authorized attacks on the ships of Spain. Other nobles contributed money for the purchase of cannon and other costly weapons. In time skilled commanders began to emerge from among the Sea Beggars' ranks, and what had been random harassment now took on a sense of purpose. On April 1, 1572, one noble, the Baron of Lumey, led an attack on the Spanish-held port of Brielle. The city fell—and the patriots acquired a base.

For England, whose uneasy alliance with Spain was beginning to unravel, the Dutch rebellion represented an opportunity. If the insurrection could be protracted, Spain would have neither money nor ships nor men to mount the expected attack on England. And so, though officially denying the fact, Queen Elizabeth tacitly gave aid to the rebels, offering them safe haven in her Channel ports and a ready market for their booty. These policies paid off in an unexpected fashion, producing a shift in naval power that would have dire consequences for the Spanish Empire.

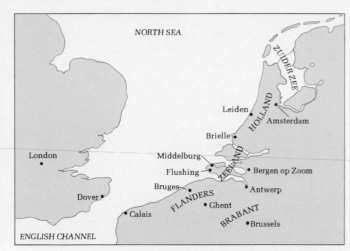

The jagged shoreline of the Netherlands provided perfect ambuscade for the Sea Beggars, who operated in shallow-draft flyboats. Rock outcroppings and islands concealed their craft; shoals and shallows blocked pursuit by deep-draft warships; and a wealth of rivers gave the Beggars access to the interior for raiding Spanish strongholds.

Astride a spirited charger, Admiral von Lumey leads the Sea Beggars into Brielle. Though they are idealized in smart military formation in this contemporary engraving, the Beggars in fact had neither uniforms nor siege equipment, and were forced to batter open the gate to the city with a piece of a mast.

During the battle of the Zuider Zee in October 1573, the Sea Beggars overrun the Spanish flagship Inquisición, while other warships blunder helplessly into the shallows. The battle—the first strictly naval engagement of the Dutch revolt—gave the Beggars clear hegemony over the vital waterway and stopped the flow of goods into Amsterdam, the center of wealth in the northern Netherlands.

Greatly outnumbered, the Sea Beggars
set upon a Spanish supply fleet as it leaves
the port of Bergen op Zoom in January
1574. In just two hours of ferocious hand-
to-hand fighting, the Beggars sank or
took 15 ships and sent to the bottom tons
of supplies needed by the besieged
Spanish garrison at Middelburg (below).

The Beggars triumphantly enter
Middelburg in February 1574, concluding
a 21-month siege that had brought the
populace to the brink of starvation. Some
of the inhabitants died from gorging
themselves on the abundant provisions
that the patriots quickly supplied.

Rebels on the rise

Until the year 1574 there were few long-lasting gains for either side in the Dutch rebellion. The Spaniards, although disciplined, ably led and well equipped, lacked the manpower necessary to deal with so persistent a foe. On many occasions they would win a town back from the Beggars, only to abandon it in order to fight elsewhere. The rebels would then quickly reoccupy it—only to lose it again when the Spaniards returned.

During the early years, however, the insurgents steadily became stronger and more organized. Calvinism was rapidly winning adherents, particularly among the merchants in the northern provinces of Holland and Zeeland,

and many new converts flocked to the rebel cause, thus uniting the middle class and the noblemen in a common determination to strike a blow against the Catholicism of Spain.

At sea, the Baron of Lumey led the Beggars in a trio of victories at Bergen op Zoom, Middelburg and Leiden in 1574. Together, these battles represented a watershed; never again would the servants of King Philip II be in control of the territory north of the Scheldt River. And even more ominous for the Spanish King, the cities south of the Scheldt, in the traditionally Catholic provinces of Flanders and Brabant, began to declare themselves for the rebels' cause.

Attacked by Sea Beggars in oar-powered barges, Spaniards abandon the redoubts from which they besieged the rebel city of Leiden. Lacking an army strong enough to relieve the months-long siege by land, William of Orange ordered sluices opened and dikes cut along two nearby rivers, thus flooding the area surrounding Leiden and making possible the waterborne attack.

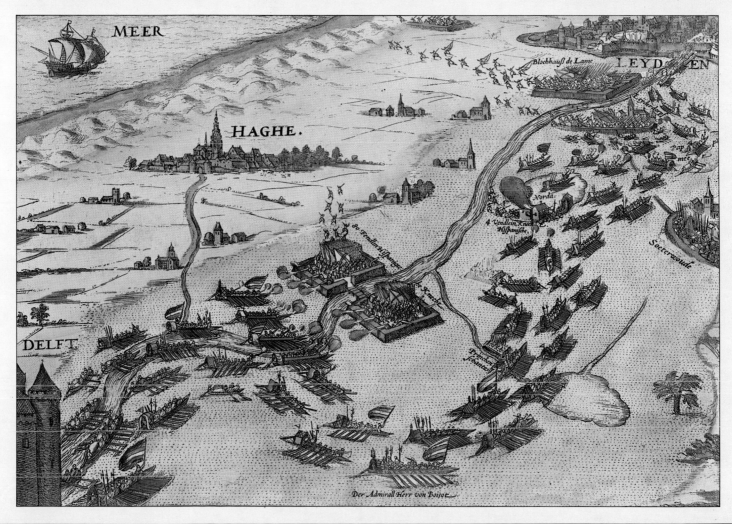

A pair of Sea Beggars' fire ships—
nicknamed "hell-burners"—blow up on
the Scheldt River, destroying a bridge
and raining explosives on Spanish ships
and troops besieging the city of
Antwerp. Though the hell-burners slowed
the attackers only temporarily, they so
terrorized Philip's sailors that three years
later the mere sight of fire ships caused
panic when the Armada stood off England.

Bedecked with rebel banners, the
optimistically named Fin de la Guerre—
"End of the War"—celebrates her
launch with a gun salute on the Scheldt
in 1585. The ship was built at a cost
of 100,000 florins (the citizens of Antwerp
footed the bill); when she ran aground
before making so much as a nick in
the Spanish forces, she came to be known
mockingly as the "Money Waster."

Spanish moves and English countermoves

As the Dutch rebellion gained momentum, Philip angrily replaced one governor general after another. In 1578, he finally found the right man in Alexander Farnese, Duke of Parma and son of the regent Margaret. By using a policy that combined diplomacy toward Catholics and hard fighting against Protestants, Parma wooed or subdued a succession of provinces, until by August 1585 the entire area of the Netherlands south of the Scheldt River had been returned to Church and King.

Elizabeth, worried by the gains of the Spanish and now no longer shrinking from open war, dispatched 6,000 troops under Robert Dudley, Earl of Leicester, to stop Parma from further advances. This intervention breathed new life into the flagging revolt. It was only a matter of time before the Beggars became a full-fledged national fighting force—an army on land, and a navy at sea.

Flying the Cross of St. George— patron saint of English warriors—a fleet under the Earl of Leicester arrives triumphantly at Flushing on the Scheldt in 1585, bringing the first overt English aid to the Dutch cause, and with it the first admission of enmity toward Spain.

Chapter 2

Mobilizing the fleets

he royal dockyard at Chatham, where the Medway River bends toward the Thames estuary and so out to sea, throbbed with activity throughout August 1586. Boatswains shouted orders, halyards creaked in blocks, oars dipped, towlines snapped taut with a spray of waterdrops. Everything seemed to be happening at once. Stacks of cordage, kegs of tallow, bolts of sailcloth and tons of produce littered the quays. Shore crews loaded supplies into oared lighters for transport to the galleons moored in the river. Caissons of shot and powder rolled up from the ordnance depot at the Tower of London, and their contents were hurried out to the ships. In the harbor, crewmen loaded various foodstuffs into the waiting holds. There were casks of salt beef and fish, of fresh apples and pears, of butter and cheese, of foamy brown beer. Aboard one vessel came a bleating, grunting platoon of sheep and piglets—meat on the hoof for the ship's cook.

In the year and two months since the *Primrose* had returned home with news of Spain's seizure of the English grain ships, England had been feverishly building up a navy. It now possessed five new or totally refurbished warships, and they were about to put to sea for a cruise that would test their sailing qualities. With the retinue of armed merchantmen, victualers, patrol and dispatch pinnaces, the fleet would total 18 sail. It would be the largest display of royal naval force since Sir William Wynter's trip to Ireland nearly seven years before. The commander, the man who was turning the hubbub into a well-orchestrated mobilization, was John Hawkins.

Several years had passed since Hawkins had gone to sea. Ever since his brief fling at international espionage in 1571, when he had helped abort the Italian banker Roberto Ridolfi's plot to overthrow Queen Elizabeth, Hawkins had expended his energies ashore, on a matter of high consequence to the realm. First as a merchant based in Plymouth, then as treasurer and chief officer of the Navy Board in Chatham, he brought about a spectacular reform of Her Majesty's navy.

When Hawkins first turned his attention to it in the 1570s, the navy was a far cry from the navy of the glory days under Henry VIII. England had then maintained upward of 50 ships in fighting trim; together they formed the most powerful maritime force in Europe. Since that time, the size of the fleet had declined by at least half. Thus diminished, the force was sufficient only to patrol England's home waters—the Channel, the North Sea and the Irish Sea. Most Englishmen—concurring with the sentiment phrased in an old couplet, "Kepe then the sea that is the wall of England / And then is England kept by Goddes hand"—thought that was enough.

Hawkins thought otherwise. He saw that if England was to compete with Spain in foreign trade—much less be ready for the war that everyone expected—then England's fleet needed improvement. It must have stronger, sleeker, handier vessels, and more of them.

Most frontline warships of the day were broad-beamed, lumbering vessels of 600 to 800 tons, dominated fore and aft by enormous castellated superstructures. These castles resembled nothing so much as floating siege towers, which was precisely what they were. They served as plat-

Dressed in armor and grasping a musket, Sir Francis Drake—"England's most renowned knight," as he is styled in the Latin inscription above him—faces the battle ahead, while crewmen load a warship with munitions. As England moved toward the confrontation with Catholic Spain, Protestants all over Europe shared the sentiment expressed in the German text of this engraving—that the "enemy follows in the devil's path."

forms from which fighting men would rain down a brutal assortment of small-arms fire onto the deck of a grappled enemy ship, while companies of foot soldiers stormed aboard the opposing vessel to engage the defenders in hand-to-hand combat. Besides their practical function, the castles gave the attacker a keen psychological edge; they brought ''majesty and terror to the enemy.'' Or so the current wisdom went.

To Hawkins, with his practical experience at sea, that was dubious. At San Juan de Ulúa in 1569, though he had lost the fight against the Spaniards, he had drawn a valuable lesson for the future. Standing up to overwhelming odds, he had shot it out with the entire Spanish West Indies fleet and sunk two mighty Spanish galleons in less than an hour. Then the wind had come up, allowing Hawkins to slip away, leaving the Spanish fleet behind him in the harbor. The episode clearly demonstrated that a seaman with good guns and a nimble vessel could best an enemy vessel without recourse to grappling and boarding. In Hawkins' view, the towering castles were an encumbrance to such an approach to

On this stylized 16th Century map, 18 warships lie in the royal dockyards at Chatham (lower left), where John Hawkins, as treasurer of the Navy Board, refurbished the fleet beginning in 1578. Chatham was an ideal place for the royal dockyards; it had easy access to the Channel via the Thames estuary—but was guarded from enemy intrusion by a string of protective forts all along the way.

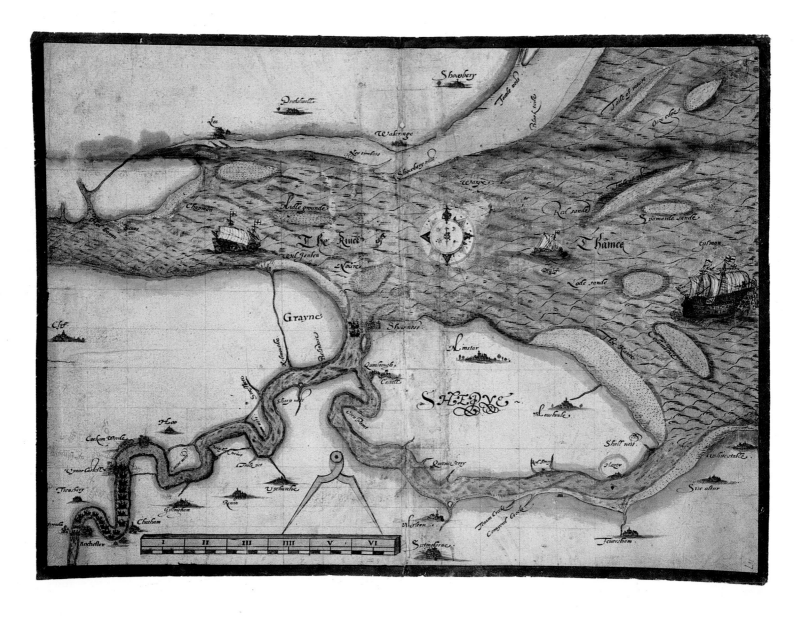

fighting. They made a ship top-heavy, reduced speed, prevented the ship from sailing handily to windward, and rendered a vessel all but unmanageable in rough weather.

Ship design was already evolving in the direction of lower lines; the 450-ton *Revenge*, destined to be one of the most famous ships of the century, was built with reduced castles when she was laid down in 1575, and she was proving fast and weatherly. When Hawkins came to the Navy Board in 1578, he determined that the Queen must have more ships like the *Revenge*. Building a brand-new fleet was not an affordable proposition, but much could be done to refurbish the ships already on hand. And so Hawkins ordered that whenever a ship came into the Chatham yard for reconditioning she should have major surgery in addition to the usual scraping, calking, tarring, painting and repair work.

One by one, beginning in 1578, the royal ships were remodeled in accordance with his instructions. The superstructure was lopped off. The sterncastle was trimmed to a gracefully sloping quarter-deck and half-deck arrangement, and the forecastle became a simple deckhouse abaft the stempost. The hull became longer in proportion to its beam, taking on a cleaner, sleeker shape above water and below, and making possible a smoother, faster passage through the water. Hawkins also made a key refinement in the rig; he had the sails recut to make them less prone to billowing. From years of trial and error at sea, he must have discovered that the flatter the sails, the closer to the direction of the wind a ship could head.

Predictably, the work at Chatham yard raised a round of protest from Hawkins' fellow board members. Some of the loudest came from William Borough, a hidebound traditionalist who was Clerk of the Ships, a scholar of navigational science and the author of a highly regarded work on compass variation. Borough complained bitterly about Hawkins' cutting down and defacing the ships. Without the lofty superstructures, Borough pointed out, the rebuilt galleons would be vulnerable to boarding from an enemy's castellated ships. In this he was right. But Hawkins had no intention of letting his galleons be boarded. The whole object was to make them able to outmaneuver any ship afloat.

The extra length that Hawkins had given the ships enabled them to carry more and bigger guns, and Hawkins made sure that his galleons bristled with armament that represented the finest of the 16th Century foundryman's art. Among the wide variety of weapons that he mounted were snub-nosed demicannon capable of hurling 32-pound iron shot, and squat cannon perriers that disgorged 24-pound stoneshot; either projectile could pierce a hull of sturdy oak. Both cannon could also heave a variety of other missiles—fragmented stone, musket balls, iron bars and chains; these, coming in a deadly hail, were for shredding sails and slashing rigging. Most notable were the slender, long-barreled cast bronze culverins and demiculverins. They hurled 17-pound and nine-pound iron balls respectively—and had a theoretical range of a mile. On these ship-battering beauties Hawkins put the highest value; together they represented more than half of the total armament he mounted.

Such were the ships that Hawkins led out of Chatham yard in September 1586, on his test run of the new navy. His flagship, a vintage 500-

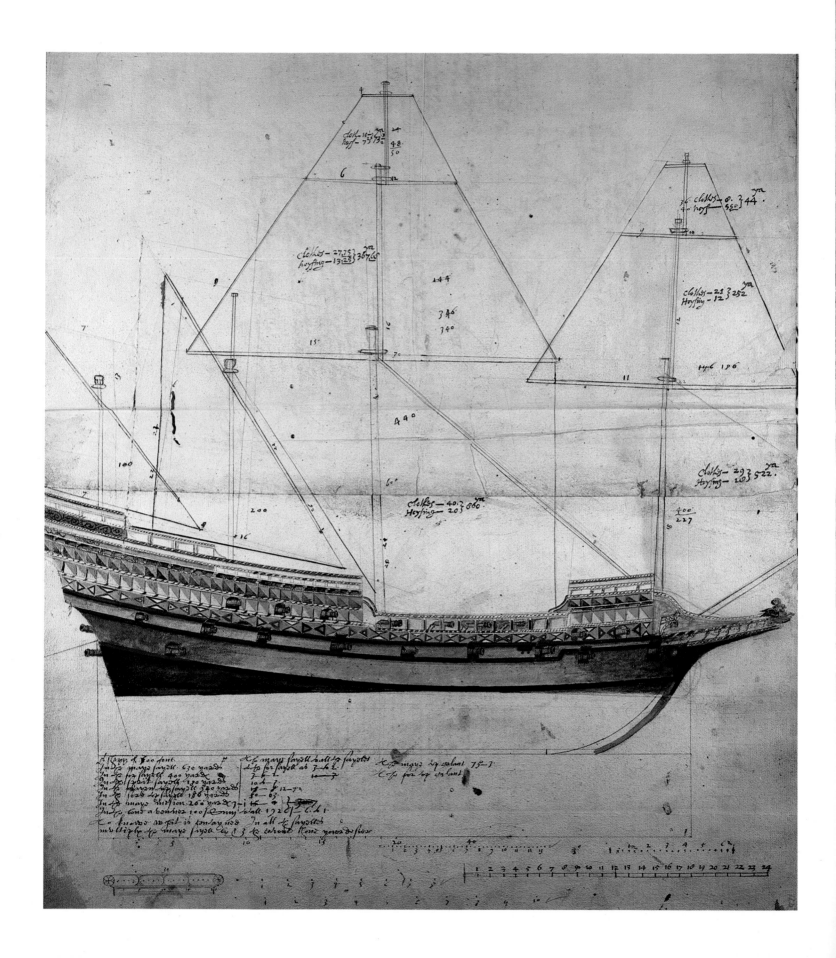

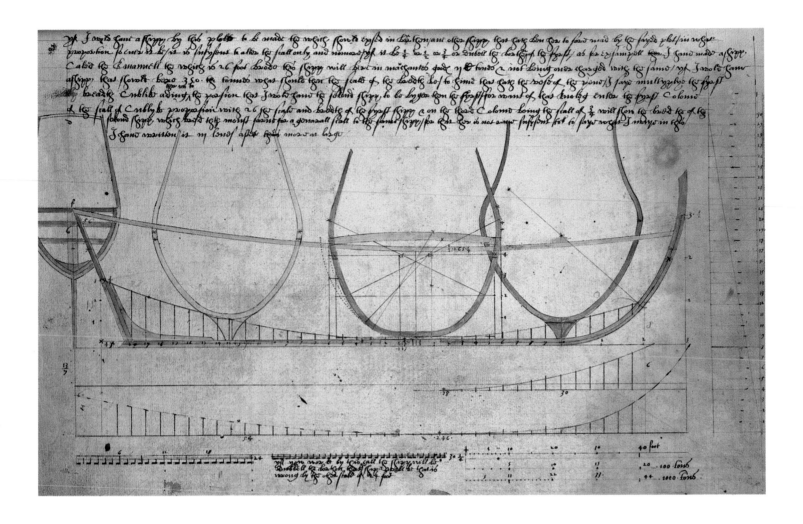

Two 16th Century drawings thought to be by Matthew Baker, master shipwright of the royal dockyards, show a broadside view of a race-built galleon and its sail plan (left), and four midship sections together with instructions for computing the dimensions of similar ships in different sizes (above). Such plans were a novelty and speeded the refurbishing of the Elizabethan navy; formerly ships had been built by lore passed from father to son, and innovation was rare.

tonner dating from the reign of Queen Mary, had been totally rebuilt and given a new name: the *Nonpareil*. She wore a new set of sails, carried a crew of some 250, and boasted 44 heavy brass guns. The fleet's second-in-command was none other than the skeptical William Borough, sailing in the *Golden Lion*, a rebuilt galleon sporting 54 guns that were deployed in two tiers along each broadside and in gunports bow and stern. Borough was out to see if the treasurer's innovations really worked. Then came the 450-ton *Revenge*, the ship used as the prototype for Hawkins' renovations. The 600-ton *Hope*, another Hawkins remake, and the spanking-new *Tremontana*, 150 tons, filled out the quintet of Queen's ships. All were resplendently gilded on the transom with the Queen's arms, and their upper works were gaily trimmed—many in green and white, the Tudor colors. All were as lavishly stocked and neatly scrubbed as wise planning and honest sweat could make them.

Crewmen had been rounded up at quaysides and waterfront ale houses throughout England (the Queen did not keep a standing corps of personnel), and had been issued money to cover travel to Chatham and the purchase of canvas sea jackets. In an effort to attract experienced sailors, Hawkins had raised the seamen's pay from six shillings eight pence to 10 shillings a month.

Quite possibly it was Hawkins' intention to blockade a Spanish port as part of his test of the navy's abilities. No one knows, because his original sailing orders have not survived. Perhaps he meant to intercept the silver fleet returning from the Caribbean, or Portuguese carracks on their way home from the East Indies. In any event, he took his ships in the general direction of Spain.

He missed both the plate ships and the carracks; all that he managed to seize was some small traders sailing in from Brazil with cargoes of sugar and dyewood. He showed the captains around his fleet—treating them to a sobering preview of the adversary their future Armada would face— and then sent them, awe-struck, on to Spain, where they circulated reports of English naval might. Then he returned to England.

If the navy's achievement on this trip was less than glamorous, it was nevertheless worthwhile: The Queen's fleet had passed its sea trials with flying colors. In some two months away from home, the ships sprang barely a leak, and the crews stayed healthy and high-spirited. William Borough decided he liked the new-style galleons after all, and he became a staunch ally of Hawkins.

When Hawkins returned to England in November, he found the country in an uproar over yet another plot to depose Queen Elizabeth. The plot— exposed not long before Hawkins' departure—included a cluster of important figures, most notably Mary Queen of Scots, Elizabeth's cousin. Among the others were Anthony Babington, a young Catholic nobleman who was an admirer of Mary's, and the Duke of Guise, her cousin, who was amassing an army across the Channel in Normandy—as if to march on England with the object of installing Mary on the throne. In Hawkins' absence Parliament had called for an investigation, tried Mary and found her guilty, and urged Elizabeth to order her execution. The English Queen temporized for the next two months; she had dealt with earlier schemes for enthroning Mary by merely reprimanding her cousin, and hoped to do the same again. But this time public pressure was too great. She was finally persuaded by her counselors to sign the death warrant on February 11, 1587.

Mary's execution a week later, on February 18, sent shock waves of indignation across Catholic Europe. In the course of the two decades during which she had stood fast for her religion against the pragmatic Protestantism of her cousin the Queen, Mary Stuart had come to be a living symbol of piety under siege, a beacon of Catholic faith in a heretic land. As heir apparent to Elizabeth, she had embodied a promise that the day would come when England would surely return to the fold of Catholicism. Now that Mary's blood was spilled in martyrdom, Catholic hearts cried out for vengeance.

Nowhere were the cries more insistent than in Spain. It was commonly said that, some years before her death, Mary Stuart had willed to Philip her rights to the sovereignty of England and Scotland. For 20 years various supplicants and advisers had urged Philip not to wait, but to undertake a seaborne invasion of England; over the years the proposition had taken on the code name "Enterprise of England." In 1583, Philip's premier admiral, the Marquis of Santa Cruz, had called for the assembly

Clutching a crucifix that proclaims her a Catholic in a land of Protestants, Mary Queen of Scots kneels before her executioner as grim-faced spectators look on and servants in the courtyard burn her garments to prevent them from being seized as curiosities. Her beheading on the 18th of February, 1587, ended Catholic hopes that she might succeed the childless Elizabeth and return England to the Church of Rome.

of a great armada that would put England back in Catholic hands. Successive commanders in the Netherlands had suggested preemptive strikes across the Channel. The present general, the brilliant Alexander Farnese, Duke of Parma, proposed ferrying 34,000 troops across in a single night, under cover of darkness. (When Pope Sixtus V learned of this scheme, he offered to contribute one million ducats from the Vatican coffers, payable the moment the first Spanish soldier touched foot on an English beach.)

Now, on the death of Mary Stuart, Philip's Ambassador to Paris, Bernardino de Mendoza, long an outspoken advocate of war with England, sent the King an urgent dispatch reminding him of Mary's will and beseeching him to act. "I pray that Your Majesty will hasten the Enterprise of England to the earliest possible date," Mendoza wrote, "for it would seem to be God's obvious design to bestow upon Your Majesty the crowns of these two kingdoms."

For 20 years Philip had met all such suggestions with impassive circumspection. "In so great an enterprise as that of England," he would say, "it is fitting to move with feet of lead." That attitude had provoked the irascible Pope Sixtus to mutter that the emperor of half the world was defied by a woman who was queen of half an island.

Philip's lack of ardor was variously attributed to prudence, to fear, to simple procrastination. He held on to important papers, one aide complained, "till they wilted." In this instance, Philip had had good reason

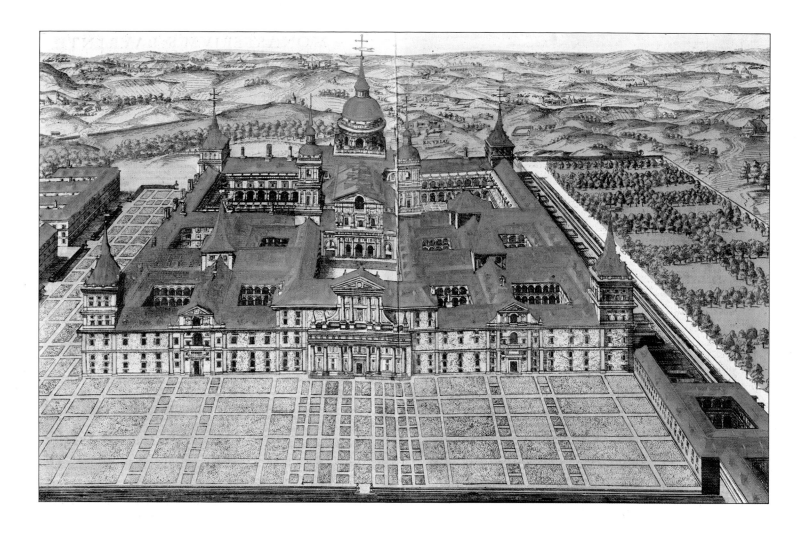

to delay. Mary Stuart had been half French by birth, and she was closely tied to France's most powerful military family. France and Spain were bitter rivals. In the face of these facts, Mary Stuart, in spite of her unswerving devotion to the cause of the Catholic church, was of dubious value to Philip; any invasion that put her on the throne of England would also have put control of the country within the grasp of Philip's oldest adversary, France.

Until now, that is. With Mary dead, the threat from France was effectively removed. The Enterprise, if successful, would bring England free and clear into the Spanish Empire.

Thus King Philip, in his monkish chambers in El Escorial, poring over reports and correspondence, weighing politics and religion, must finally have concluded. For on the evening of March 31, 1587, the monastery's inner sanctum suddenly began to hum with energy. He drafted and sent out a volley of directives and urgent inquiries. The squadrons of ships at Cartagena and Málaga must hurry to Lisbon. The arsenals at Barcelona and Naples must release all spare ordnance to the Atlantic fleet. Where was the consignment of saltpeter from Genoa, and why was it late? Could the Pope be persuaded to advance his million ducats immediately? And to Santa Cruz, in command of the Atlantic fleet at

Above the mountain village of El Escorial, 31 miles from Madrid, the monastic fortress of San Lorenzo rises stark and impregnable—enclosing a gridlike arrangement of 4,000 rooms, 86 staircases and 100 miles of corridors. Except for the basilica dome and the gables, every line within and without was as unbending as the temperament of King Philip, who ordered the edifice built.

Lisbon, went an abrupt and crucial order: Mobilize your armada, and be ready to sail before the end of spring. The Enterprise of England had officially begun.

The invasion plan, as Philip conceived it, would distill the best ideas of his two most brilliant commanders—the Marquis of Santa Cruz by sea, and the Duke of Parma by land. The admiral's proposal—a fleet of 510 vessels to sail from Lisbon with a landing force of 64,000 troops—presumed a strictly naval operation that would have Santa Cruz himself in charge. As presented, it was just too ambitious and expensive. Parma's scheme—a rapier-like infantry thrust across the Channel—would be less cumbersome. He already stood poised in Flanders with an army of highly disciplined German, Walloon, Spanish and Italian mercenaries who had never lost a pitched battle. Barges for moving the troops to England could easily be constructed. Reinforcements could be brought up swiftly through northern Europe. There was just one hitch. Success would depend on total surprise—otherwise the troop barges would never get past the ubiquitous Dutch flyboats, much less the obliterating guns of the English warships. "Hardly possible!" Philip had noted in the margin of Parma's suggestion.

Both plans were flawed, but both held exciting promise. Why not deliver a direct frontal assault with Parma's veterans, but, instead of attempting surprise, bring in Santa Cruz to hold off the English fleet? The admiral would gather a force of top-line fighting ships at Lisbon—not in the numbers he wanted, but still a respectable armada—and steer for England. Parma's troops, massed at Nieuport and Dunkirk on the Flemish coast, would set out on signal in their barges. There would be a mid-Channel rendezvous, and the admiral's armada would escort the general's flotilla to a landing site somewhere in the Thames estuary. Santa Cruz would also bring troops of his own, but his main task would be to convoy Parma's forces and to secure supply lines to the mainland.

The scheme was ingenious; it called for deftness, precision, and full cooperation between two headstrong but skilled commanders. But it had to be put into effect soon, without delay, while all of Europe was crying out for it to happen.

The first concern was to boost the Atlantic fleet to fighting strength. The ships at Lisbon were hauled and calked and smeared with tallow. Shipments of spars, sailcloth, hemp and tackle moved down from the Baltic. Contracts were sent out for biscuit, rice, dried fish, olive oil, gunpowder and shot. Sailors were recruited, new companies of infantry raised. And in harbors all along the Atlantic coast, from Biscay to Andalusia, ships began to gather in clusters. There were tall Portuguese galleons, heavily gunned merchant ships, galleys from Naples, *urcas* (supply hulks), and small craft, all in various conditions of seaworthiness and repair. Slowly and creakily, with much noise and confusion, the unwieldy process of mobilization began to take place.

Philip wanted the Armada ships to make their rendezvous at Lisbon by June at the latest, and then to set sail for England early in the summer. Considering the general inertia of the Spanish bureaucracy, and the enormous amount of fitting-out and provisioning the fleet would require, his timetable seems brashly optimistic. In any case, in midspring

In a windowless chamber lighted by an oil lamp, the worn chair where Philip sat as he made plans for the invasion of England stands beside a writing table. Together with an adjoining bedroom and private chapel, this spartan cell in the massive fortress at El Escorial constituted Philip's everyday world; here he took his meals, received his ministers and dispatched commands across his far-flung dominion.

an event occurred in Cádiz that set back the launching a full 12 months.

As the major port on Spain's southern coast, Cádiz was one of the most important staging areas for the Armada. By now it was crammed with shipping. More than 60 vessels rode at anchor in the roadstead—merchantmen from the Mediterranean, coastal traders awaiting a fair wind that would carry them north to France and Germany, wine ships taking on casks from nearby Jerez, West Indian merchantmen fitting out for the next Atlantic crossing. There was a 1,000-ton Biscayan ready to head west with nails, barrel hoops and horseshoes for Philip's colonists, and a 700-ton Levantine vessel that had recently returned from the New World with wool, hides and logwood. The harbor also contained some Dutch cargo hulks that had been impounded for use in the Armada, and various other naval supply ships and freighters. And in a shallow bay upstream rode a tall new galleon just arrived from the Biscay shipyards to take on guns and soldiers for the Marquis of Santa Cruz.

An air of fiesta pervaded the town of Cádiz itself, situated on the gentle limestone promontory that overlooked the entrance to the harbor. Sailors on shore leave strutted about the waterfront, here and there stopping to watch an acrobat turning cartwheels in the town square. Wine shops did a sprightly business. A company of strolling players staged a *comedia*. Palm trees swayed in a southwest breeze, and the April sun flashed down on the red tile roofs of the whitewashed houses. The scent of orange blossoms filled the air of Andalusia, and the sierra was bright with wild flowers.

All of a sudden, around four in the afternoon on Wednesday, April 29, a line of ships appeared on the northwest horizon and stood in toward the harbor. They carried no identifying flags or insignia, and thus caused some lively speculation as to just whose ships they might be. A squadron of six galleys rowed out to meet them.

As the ships bore steadily in toward the entrance to the harbor, a puff of gun smoke burst ominously from the prow of the leading vessel. Trumpets brayed, and the red-and-white banners of St. George broke from the mastheads. They were seven English galleons, and they were followed by a like number of armed merchantmen and a train of supplementary craft, come to raid and pillage. On the quarter-deck of the flagship there strode a short, barrel-chested figure with a round face, a brown beard and cheeks as ruddy as crab apples. He was the most celebrated seaman of the 16th Century, a man whose fame had penetrated to every hamlet of the Spanish Empire: the daredevil Francis Drake. No other name commanded such terror or respect among the Spaniards, who called him the "master thief of the unknown world." The stories about Drake had assumed a quality of legend: No prize could escape him; he commanded the winds; in his cabin hung a magic mirror that showed the position of every Spanish ship, at any given moment, anywhere on the high seas. In fact, there was no private individual who had done more damage to Spanish fortunes and prestige.

Drake's most recent exploit, in 1585, had been particularly galling. It was during the period when a number of English grain ships had been impounded in Spanish ports, and Queen Elizabeth had given him a commission to take reprisals. Take them he did, with a vengeance. Drake

Outside the walled city of Cádiz, at the tip of the peninsula sheltering the harbor from the Atlantic Ocean, fishermen haul netted tuna ashore. In the 16th Century, Cádiz was a major staging and provisioning base for Spanish treasure fleets and the warships of the Armada.

had steered straight for Spain's northwest coast, to the port of Vigo. He had stayed there a week, commandeering provisions and throwing the inhabitants into a panic. Never before had a hostile English fleet dared insult the Spaniards right in their home waters.

From Vigo, Drake had sailed west to the Caribbean, stopping en route at the Cape Verde Islands to sack and incinerate the towns of Santiago and Porto Praya. Reaching the Indies, he had stormed the fortified city of Santo Domingo and extracted 25,000 ducats in ransom. Next he had ransacked Cartagena, capital of the Spanish Main, holding it up for another 110,000 ducats and capturing some 60 cannon from the city's fortifications. News of these doings had caused major turmoil in Europe's financial circles. Philip's credit rating had plunged so low he could not raise the money to pay his troops in Flanders. "The Bank of Seville is broke, the Bank of Valencia also very likely," crowed Lord Burghley, Elizabeth's chief minister. "Truly, Sir Francis Drake is a fearful man to the King of Spain."

When intelligence agents had brought England news of the sudden activity in Spanish ports in 1587, Drake had reacted swiftly. "Give me a fleet and a free hand, and I will smoke the wasps out of their nests," he had bragged, and, yielding to his importuning, Queen Elizabeth had obliged him. He had sailed from Plymouth on April 12, 1587, in a tremendous rush, with orders from the Queen "to impeach the purpose of the Spanish fleet and stop their meeting at Lisbon." Those orders amounted to royal approval of John Hawkins' aggressive naval strategy.

Drake was carrying the battle to Spanish waters, as Hawkins had presumably hoped to do in his recent sea trials.

And, not incidentally, Drake would take what he could in the way of Spanish prizes. This expedition, like most of Drake's earlier ones, blended official navy operations with commercial privateering. Everyone expected it to make a profit—including the Queen. She was, in fact, a principal shareholder; she provided four galleons, 400 to 500 tons in size, all recently built or remodeled according to Hawkins' specifications. Drake himself supplied a galleon and some pinnaces, as did Charles Lord Howard of Effingham, Lord High Admiral of England. Besides these, an association of London shipowners had sent seven heavily armed merchantmen. Along with some other privateers and pinnaces, the fleet comprised perhaps 23 sail, as powerful a fighting force as any it might meet in Spain just then.

Drake was so eager to get moving that when the London vessels pulled into Plymouth on April 11, he gave them only 24 hours for last-minute watering and provisioning. The next day the fleet weighed anchor. "The wind commands me away," he wrote the Queen's secretary, Sir Francis Walsingham. "Our ships are under sail. God grant we may so live in His fear as the enemy may have cause to say that God doth fight for Her Majesty as well abroad as at home. Haste! From aboard her Majesty's good ship the *Elizabeth Bonaventure*."

There was reason to hurry. At the prospect of using military force, Queen Elizabeth had an unsettling habit of changing her mind. And so she did this time, hoping at the eleventh hour to patch together a peace agreement with Philip. She sent a pinnace racing after Drake to forbid him to enter a Spanish harbor or to land on Spanish soil. The fleet was already too far ahead to be caught, however. Drake dropped down the Atlantic, pushed along by a fair southwest breeze and unaware of the Queen's second thoughts. By the afternoon of Wednesday, April 29, he had come within striking distance of Cádiz.

In his eagerness to reach Spain, Drake had made no attempt to keep his fleet in formation. The fast-sailing galleons were the first to arrive, while the slower craft were still hull down to the rear. Without waiting for the laggards, Drake summoned his vanguard captains to an immediate war council. By naval tradition that dated from the time of Henry VIII, battle plans in any campaign were decided by mutual discussion and consent among the senior officers.

Drake assembled his captains aboard the *Elizabeth Bonaventure* and simply told them what he wanted. The wind is with us, he said, the sun behind us, and by the grace of God we shall capture Cádiz before nightfall. There was no chance for debate, no detailed battle plan devised. The admiral had made up his mind.

The fleet's second-in-command, William Borough, could scarcely believe his ears. This was the same William Borough who sat on the Navy Board as Clerk of the Ships. When he was at sea he liked to operate according to protocol, certainly not in this headlong, improvised way. Half the fleet was still strung out along the horizon. Cádiz reportedly had some powerful shore batteries, and the harbor entrance was narrow and shoal. Would it not be better to wait a bit, study the charts, hold

A pocket computer for a 16th Century mariner

The myth that Sir Francis Drake had a magic mirror for locating Spaniards at sea may well have sprung from his possession of an instrument like the one below—a way-finding aid with so many functions that its name "compendium" seems like an understatement. In miniaturized form, the gadget combined many navigational tools that had been developed during preceding centuries.

This particular compendium, a masterpiece fashioned by the chief engraver of Queen Elizabeth's Royal Mint, consisted of seven layers of spinning rings, flip-up pointers and lists of inscribed data. It contained tables specifying the latitudes of major European ports, the tidal variations at those ports, and figures needed to compute a ship's latitude on the basis of noontime observations of the sun's angle above the horizon.

To determine that vertical angle, the compendium possessed a pair of rotating indicators that worked somewhat like gun sights; they could be used for horizontal sightings as well as vertical—measuring the angle between the ship's heading and a landmark or another ship, for example.

The compendium was also a versatile timekeeper. It had a sundial with a pointer that could be angled correctly for a particular latitude and would cast its shadow on a Roman numeral giving the hour of the day. To tell the time after sundown, it had a "nocturnal"—a nighttime dial with a perforation for sighting the polestar and lining it up with two movable indicators resembling the hands of a clock. An added bonus was a perpetual calendar that could not only help the seafarer keep track of the date, but would also remind him of saints' days and other religious holidays.

The marvelous miniaturization of the compendium naturally had a price. Only a limited amount of data could be compressed into the tables, and the sightings taken with the instrument were inevitably less accurate than those made with larger navigational tools. When it came to workaday navigation, not even the masterful Drake would have relied on this pocket-sized marvel. But as the myth about his mirror suggests, the compendium had value simply for show.

This 1569 gilt-and-brass navigational instrument was a handy three inches in diameter and, when folded, half an inch thick.

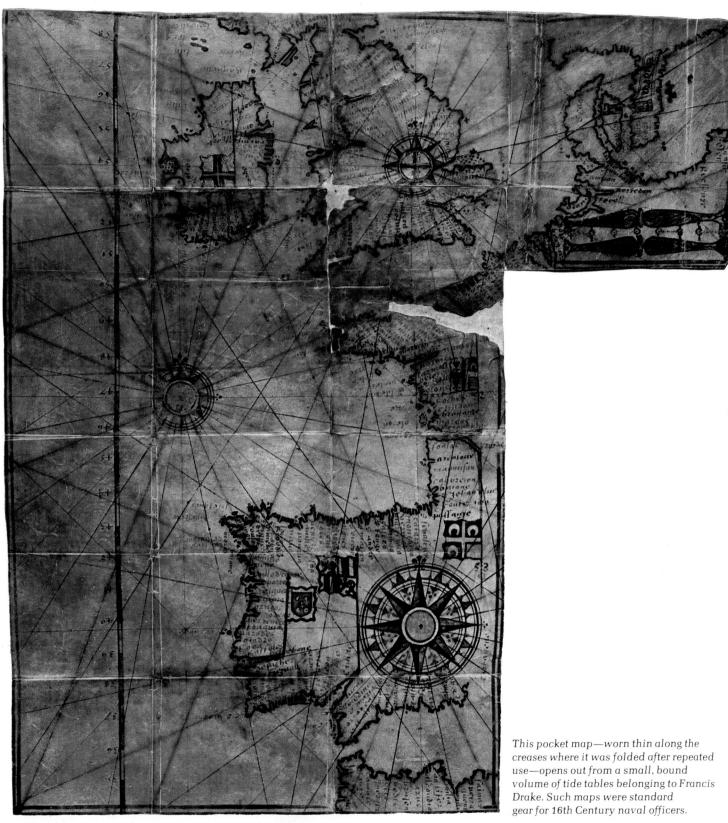

This pocket map—worn thin along the creases where it was folded after repeated use—opens out from a small, bound volume of tide tables belonging to Francis Drake. Such maps were standard gear for 16th Century naval officers.

a proper council, work out a battle plan? Borough asked reasonably.

"We shall not stay at all," Drake interrupted.

Borough climbed back aboard his own galleon, the *Golden Lion*, in considerable disgruntlement. He had no clear idea what tactics would be followed, or just what he himself was expected to do. Drake was already standing in toward Cádiz, however, and the vice admiral could only follow. The rest of the fleet scurried to catch up, in such confused order, Borough testily observed, as was unheard of in this sort of action.

To Drake, the order did not matter. The most powerful weapons, he knew, were audacity and surprise. His instinct for bold and sudden attack had bought victory in the past, and he trusted it now. The town of Cádiz rose up on its limestone hummock, the harbor behind it sprouting a thicket of masts and rigging. Drake led his galleons toward the harbor entrance, charging directly in at the squadron of galleys lined up to meet him. Without ceremony, he opened up his guns.

The Spanish galleys presented a fine martial array, low and lean in the water, their bronze bow rams glinting in the sun, uniformed warriors poised on their foredecks. They could do little to defend themselves, however. The English galleons swung broadside across their bows and poured down volley after devastating volley of great shot. Oarsmen and soldiers fell in droves under the hail of fire. There was no hope of boarding. The galleys backed off, then broke for cover, stroking furiously for a shoal area on the northeast side of the harbor.

In the Cádiz roadstead pandemonium broke loose. Most of the anchored ships carried only token crews; many had no guns, and some no sails. On vessels that could move, the crews cut their anchor cables and tried to flee. Some collided, others ran aground, while a scattering of the smaller craft found temporary safety in the shallows of the upper bay. As the English swept into the harbor, only one vessel put up a fight. The Levantine argosy, still at anchor, started blasting away from every gunport. It was a gallant gesture, but suicidal. The Queen's four galleons drew up, like wolves around a wounded stag, and summarily pounded the argosy to bits. Her 40 brass guns were still spewing fire as she gurgled to the bottom with her cargo of hides and logwood.

In the town itself, the population milled about in terrified confusion. Everyone expected the English to land troops and assault the town walls. There would be fighting in the streets, pillage and rapine. A Cádiz magistrate directed that all civilians who were too old, too young or too frail to bear arms should take refuge in the fort. The commander of the fort, heedless of the plight of the citizens as he contemplated the ships menacing the harbor, ordered the gates slammed shut. A crowd of panicky residents surged in the narrow street outside, and before the mess had been sorted out and the gates reopened, 25 women and children had been trampled to death.

The English had no intention of landing; there was far too much profit to be had in the harbor itself. Before sunset, they had taken full control. They began working methodically through the anchored ships—sorting prizes, transferring cargo, towing the emptied hulks into the channel and setting them afire. Occasional rounds from the fort and a pair of shore batteries would splash in the direction of the invader's ships, but they did no damage. The guns had been intended to repel Moorish landing parties; from their positions they could not shoot far enough to reach the main anchorage.

The plunder continued until far into the night, the English crews working by the light of the flaming hulks. By dawn the wine and biscuit and guns and other booty had been laded into English bottoms, the prizes had been taken, and the fires were dying. The English had clearly won a major victory. Borough, for one, was ready to quit.

Drake had other ideas. "There must be a beginning of any great matter," he would note later, "but the continuing on to the end, until it be thoroughly finished, yields the true glory." The great galleon of Santa Cruz still swung at her cables in the shallow upper bay, along with the small fry that had escaped from the main anchorage the evening before. Capturing or sinking the Spanish admiral's galleon would be glory indeed. Drake anchored the *Elizabeth Bonaventure* with the rest of his ships in the main harbor, and then climbed into his admiral's barge. Leading a column of pinnaces and frigates, he nosed up through the sandbars and mud flats into the upper bay.

Vice Admiral Borough, left in the main harbor aboard the *Golden Lion*, regarded his position with some trepidation. The Spaniards were dragging a heavy bronze culverin from the gates of the town to a position that overlooked the harbor, where it presented a real threat to the English ships. Furthermore, the wind was now turning fluky. If it dropped too low, the fleet would be unable to sail out of the harbor. And on top of all this, he had been given no instructions and had no notion where Drake had gone or what he intended to do next. So Borough set out in his own barge to find out.

When he reached the *Elizabeth Bonaventure*, Borough was directed to the upper bay. He arrived there to find the Santa Cruz galleon in flames, and to be told that Drake had already returned to the main harbor. Borough headed back. By the time he had regained his own vessel, the Spanish culverin had scored a direct hit—on the *Golden Lion*. Borough's galleon had been holed at the water line, and the ball had sheared off the leg of his master gunner. The wind was dying and there was no time to waste. As Borough clambered aboard his ship the master was already warping her out of range of the Spanish gun, into open water on the far side of the fleet.

The maneuver would have made good sense had it not exposed the *Golden Lion* to danger from another quarter. The six galleys, seeing a wounded, isolated enemy galleon, darted out from their refuge in the northeast shoals and began to pepper the *Lion* with shot. A squadron of galleys might be no match for a whole fleet of warships, but with an advantage of 6 to 1 they just might have won out. Drake had to send a rescue squad—the Queen's galleon *Rainbow*, half a dozen merchantmen and his own pinnace.

Thus reinforced, Borough was able to turn back the attack and send the galleys scurrying for cover. Then he edged the *Lion* out toward the harbor mouth, as if anticipating a full withdrawal from Cádiz. He need not have bothered. For now the wind died completely, leaving him immobilized in a flat, glassy calm.

An armory of wicked tools to maul a foe

When they confronted each other on the seas in the 16th Century, Spanish and English cannoneers had available to them a remarkable variety of ammunition. In addition to plain round shot—either cast-iron or stone balls—armories of the day offered the gunner a plethora of ingenious loads "to shoot down Masts, Yards, Shrouds, teare the sailes, spoile the men, or anything that is above the decks," as an English manual phrased it.

One such device was case shot—fist-sized capsules that would burst open on impact, showering lead pellets, nails or scrap metal in all directions. Another consisted of halved or quartered balls linked by iron bars and chains; they would spread apart in transit, then wrap around a mast—or a human neck—with a double wallop.

Perhaps the most lethal-looking of all the contraptions were spiked projectiles and switchblade-like missiles designed to spring open as soon as they left a cannon's muzzle—and to deliver frightful gashes when they hit their target. Developed early in the century, they were an attempt to marry an old method with a new—to deliver a blade by means of gunpowder.

Whether the spiked or bladed shot actually worked in flight is uncertain. They were in any event dangerous to use; they had to be bound with oakum-smeared canvas lest they destroy the barrel from which they were fired. But to the English at least, they seemed so potent in principle that the royal treasury was footing the bill for such missiles a full century after the Armada.

Ingenious 16th Century shot included balls equipped with either blades or spikes that folded for loading, then—theoretically—opened in flight; also shown are chain-linked balls and cartridges that were filled with shrapnel.

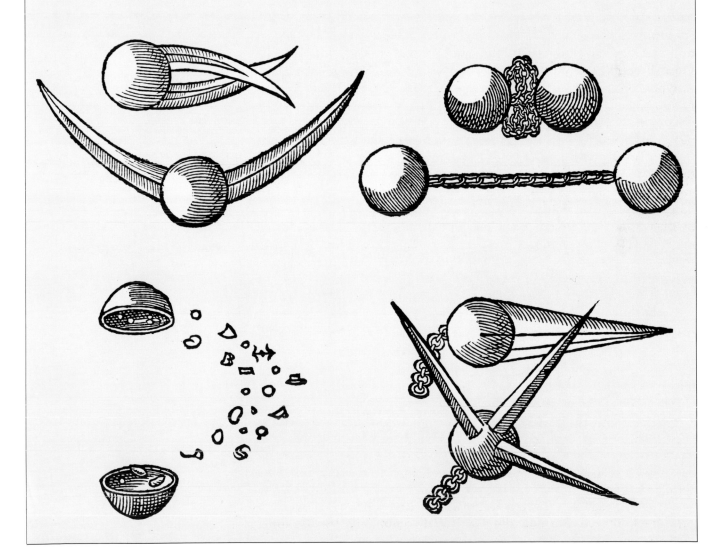

Drake himself was now ready to quit Cádiz. He had been watching the wind carefully, gambling that it would hold until he had squeezed the last ounce of spoils from the Spanish ships. But now scarcely a cat's-paw rippled the waters of Cádiz harbor. The English fleet drifted without steerageway, sails hanging listlessly from the yards. This made a dismal anticlimax to a triumphant night, and it was potentially dangerous. The English were trapped in harbor as effectively as a lion in a cage.

As the English fleet lay becalmed, the Cádiz defenders now had the advantage—and in the next 12 hours they made the best use of it they could. They set up another great gun on the shore front, aimed it directly at Drake's flagship, and started firing. Some 3,300 troops under the Duke of Medina Sidonia marched up to reinforce the town. The fort batteries continued to bark out volleys. The galleys, now the only mobile craft at Cádiz, crept from behind the shoals to pluck at the fringes of the fleet. And some small hulks anchored under the town wall were smeared with pitch, set alight and pushed out on the tide toward the English ships.

Miraculously, by some odd confluence of artful seamanship and sheer luck, the English escaped almost unscathed. With the single exception of the casualty aboard Borough's *Golden Lion*, no sailor was hurt, and not a ship was damaged. Each galley attack was stopped short with a businesslike succession of broadsides. The English crews, by laying out a system of anchors and smartly playing the cables, were able to warp their vessels around to dodge assaults or bring their own guns to bear. Men in rowboats caught the fire ships on the fly and pushed or towed them away to burn out harmlessly in the shallows. The work went on all afternoon and half the night. Finally, a little after midnight, a land breeze came up. Drake led the English fleet out of Cádiz harbor and into the open Atlantic, herding along a flock of prize ships.

It was an astonishing victory, and a brilliant opening to Drake's Iberian adventure. He claimed to have captured or sunk 37 enemy vessels, more than half the tonnage in Cádiz harbor. The Spanish authorities counted a bit less, but not by much. The casualty report to King Philip listed 24 ships destroyed, for a total value of 172,000 ducats. "The loss was not very great," the King declared, "but the daring of the attempt was very great indeed."

From this initial triumph, Drake went on to harry the shipping all along Spain's Atlantic coast over the next six weeks. "I have singed the King of Spain's beard," he gleefully declared. But beards grow back, and a few dozen ships could soon be replaced. In his report on the Cádiz raid, Drake excitedly told Secretary Walsingham, "I dare not almost write of the great forces we hear the King of Spain hath. Prepare in England strongly, and most by sea!"

Even as he wrote, more shipping destined for the Armada, and large quantities of supplies and provisions, were funneling out from Naples, Milan, Sicily, Barcelona and Cartagena on the Mediterranean, through the Strait of Gibraltar and into the port of Lisbon. Drake resolved to lurk along the Atlantic coast and grab each convoy as it rounded Cape St. Vincent and headed north. In order to do this, he wanted a land base in southern Spain or Portugal, where he would be able to take on fresh water and careen his ships.

On a map of Cádiz, small red dots and two columns of explanation track the movement of English ships through the harbor during the raid led by Sir Francis Drake in 1587. The signature "William Borough" at the lower right matches the lettering—marking the map as the handiwork of Drake's second-in-command. His ship, the Golden Lion (designated by the letter "f" in the outer harbor), was hit by a gun (keyed to the letter "m") located on the peninsula's eastern shore.

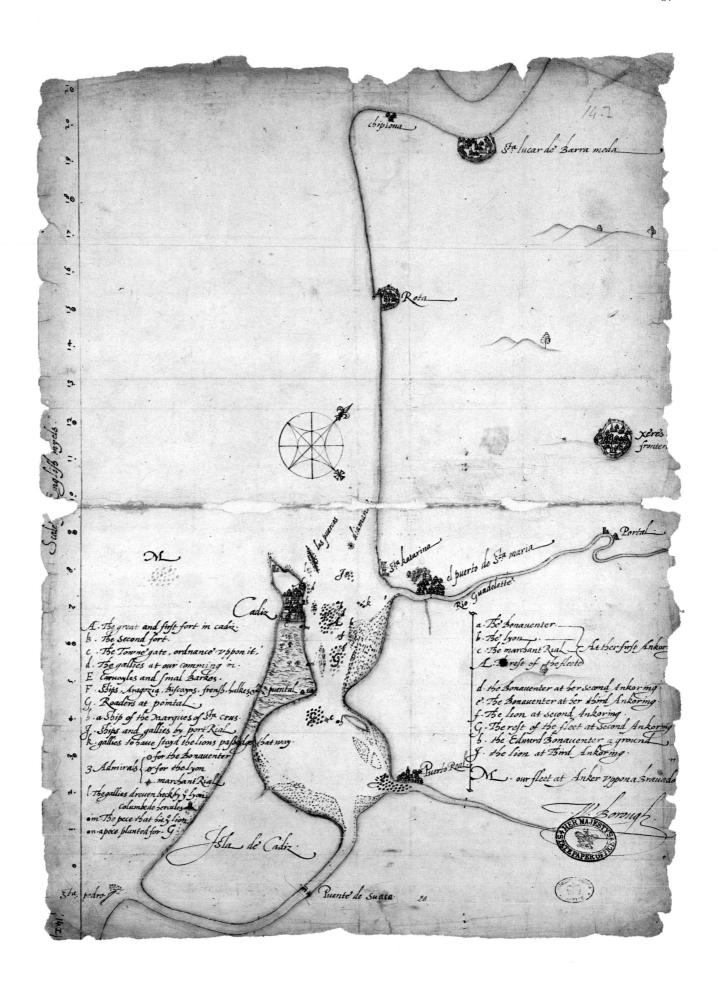

147

chipiona

Sta lucar de Barra meda

Rota

Xeres fronter

Scale English mydes

M

las puercas
diamante

Sta katarina   el puerto de Sta maria   Portal

Cadiz

Rio Guadelette

A. The great and first fort in cadiz.
b. The second fort.
c. The Towne gate, ordnance vppon it.
d. The gallies at our comming in.
E. Carauyles and smal barkos.
F. Ships, Aragoza, biscayns, frenss, hulkes, &c.
G. Roaders at pontal
h. a Ship of the marquies of Sta crus.
I. Ships and gallies by port Rial.
k. gallies to haue stayd the lions passadge that way.

⎧ o. for the Bonauenter
3 Admirals ⎨ o. for the Lyon
⎩ o. marchant Rial.

l. The gallies dreuen backby ye lyon &
        columbe de serules.
m. The pece that hit ye lion.
n. a pece planted for G.

puental

a. The Bonauenter.
b. The lyon.
c. The marchant Rial. ⎫ At ther first Ankor
A. The rest of the fleete

d. the Bonauenter at her second Ankoring
e. The Bonauenter at ser third Ankoring
f. The lion at second Ankoring
G. The rest of the fleet at second Ankoring
h. the Edward Bonauenter a ground
I. the lion at third Ankoring

Puerto Real

M. our fleet at Anker vppon a Brauado

W. Borough

Isla de Cadiz

Sta pedro

Puente de suasa   20

He summoned his captains and laid this plan before them. Since a general blockade of the Iberian coast was in fact the stated purpose of the expedition, most of the officers readily agreed—all except Vice Admiral Borough, who could find nothing in the Queen's orders that allowed for a landing on the Spanish mainland. He protested strongly, in writing. Drake would always listen to other men's opinions, a friend once said, but he always followed his own. The admiral pocketed the letter from Borough, and two days later he locked the astonished Clerk of the Ships in quarters for insubordination. He then proceeded to plant troops on the Portuguese coast.

The first English landing, at Lagos some 40 miles east of Cape St. Vincent, met with heavy resistance from the town's garrison. A hot splattering of cannon and harquebus fire drove the English back to their ships. Drake then turned west to Sagres Point, a tall headland hard by the tip of Cape St. Vincent, at the southwest corner of Iberia.

The high, windswept cliffs of Sagres Point jut south toward Africa, the ocean breaking on three sides about their feet. This is barren, lonely land, and to mariners it is hallowed. Here, almost a century and a half before Drake's time, the scholarly Portuguese Prince Henry the Navigator had built a castle and founded a library for the study of nautical science—a simple act that marked the beginning of Europe's great maritime enterprise. Sagres Point was the birthplace of the spirit that had sent the first caravels exploring down the African coast, westward into the Atlantic past the outermost edge of the known world, and eventually to the gold and spices of the East Indies, to the riches of the Caribbean, and to the exploits of such men as Drake himself. The library no longer existed. What mattered to Drake at the moment, however, was the strategic position of the cape. It guarded a small bay to the east, where he wanted to base his fleet.

Drake led a landing party of pikemen, musketeers and harquebusiers up the cliff path to the Sagres promontory. The castle, built over the cliffs on three sides and faced on the fourth by a 40-foot parapet, seemed impregnable to all but an army with siege guns. Unable to blast down the castle wall, Drake devised another stratagem. He set his marksmen to peppering the ramparts, and under this covering barrage he proceeded to stack pitch-soaked fagots against the wooden gates, laboring shoulder to shoulder beside his men. Within two hours the gates had crumbled to ashes, and the English were spraying the inner defenses with musket shot. The garrison commander, twice wounded, surrendered.

There was no need to hold the castle, but simply to knock out a threat to the anchorage below. Drake seized the defenders' weapons and let the men go. He then set torches to the castle buildings.

With his base snugly established in the lee of the Sagres cliffs, Drake led a squadron north to Lisbon, where he challenged Santa Cruz to come out and fight. The marquis, still struggling to put his fleet in order, was in no condition to accept. Ordnance that had been promised for his Portuguese galleons had failed to arrive, and he still lacked crews and soldiers. His other ships were hardly more ready for battle. He sat in fuming helplessness while Drake paraded tauntingly back and forth a few miles offshore. After a day or two of this, the English admiral caught a fresh north breeze back down to Cape St. Vincent. This was where the real business of the voyage would be done anyway.

For the next three weeks the English fleet plied the shipping lanes around the cape, methodically sweeping the ocean for cargo vessels carrying supplies from the Mediterranean to Lisbon. It made for dull, unrewarding work after the glories of Cádiz, but the effect on Spanish mobilization was devastating. "The English are masters of the sea," the Venetian Ambassador told his government. "Lisbon and the whole coast are blockaded." The quantities of guns, powder, provisions, soldiers and warships that Santa Cruz so sorely lacked simply did not arrive. Convoys that were heading out past Gibraltar would stop short at Cádiz, or turn back to Málaga. Of the vessels that tried to run the English gantlet—most of them small barks and caravels of under 60 tons—Drake captured or destroyed considerably more than 100.

The principal cargo turned out to be 1,700 tons of hoops and barrel staves, intended for building the casks that would hold the water and provisions for the Armada. Drake burned the lot. Because the wood in provisions casks had to be seasoned in order to prevent spoilage of the contents, the loss of the staves would severely cripple the Spaniards. And this was not all. Drake played havoc with the Portuguese tuna fishery, systematically destroying both the nets and the fishing boats— thereby knocking out the supply of salt tuna that formed the main protein staple of the Spanish fleet.

The blockade continued unopposed, but the work was beginning to tell on the English fleet. Ships grew foul with steady use, and crews began falling to scurvy and other shipboard ills. Furthermore, while the blockade thoroughly demoralized the Spaniards, it was yielding the English no marketable prizes. The average seaman shipped with Drake not for patriotism, not for glory, and hardly for the Queen's 10 shillings a month. He hoped to get deliriously rich on his share of looted treasure. Drake himself began to feel the need for "some little comfortable dew of heaven, some crowns or some reasonable booties." A logical place to look for them would be in the Azores, where King Philip's treasure ships stopped to water before the last run home.

Intelligence agents told him that a huge East India carrack out of Goa was due in the Azores any day now, and on June 1, Drake set out to find it. He closed down the base at Sagres, sent the sick crewmen home to their families via the Cádiz prizes, and steered straight for the Azores with his fleet. On the way, a gale blew up from the south and roared for 48 hours, dispersing the ships. A number of them, including the entire London contingent, were driven back to England. The rest of the fleet reformed—all except one galleon. The Golden Lion broke away to chase an unidentified sail, and instead of rejoining the fleet held steadily north and disappeared over the horizon. Drake was furious. He was convinced that William Borough, who had spent the entire blockade under lock and key in his cabin aboard the Lion, had regained control and ordered the ship's defection. Drake convened a court-martial and sentenced Borough to death in absentia for mutiny and treason—charges that Borough's friends on the Navy Board preferred to dismiss after the Clerk of the Ships reached England.

Drake's squadron, now reduced to six galleons and some pinnaces, sighted the island of São Miguel in the Azores on June 18. The commander bore in toward the land, and there, under the steep gray cliffs, could be seen the sails of an enormous vessel. It was the Portuguese ship *San Felipe*, the very East India carrack he had come to find. Carracks were among the largest ships afloat in the 16th Century, and the *San Felipe* must have displaced some 1,400 tons. She was loaded to her gunwales, with cargo overflowing onto her decks, blocking her gunports. She surrendered with scarcely a fight.

Drake had captured the single richest prize of his swashbuckling career, one of the grandest hauls of the century. The *San Felipe* carried an imperial fortune in pepper, cloves, cinnamon and other spices, in silks and calico, in indigo and ivory, in gold, silver and caskets of gem stones. The total worth came to £114,000, more than three times the value of all the goods and shipping captured or destroyed at Cádiz. The Queen took £40,000 as her share, Drake £17,000, and the rest was split among officers, crew members and other shareholders. At a time when the Navy Board under Hawkins' direction spent £6,000 a year, Drake had brought home more than enough money to underwrite England's defense against any impending invasion. The capture also gave another hard knock to Philip's credit rating, further delaying his preparations for the Armada.

As Drake sped home to riches and acclaim, the Spanish fleet languished at Lisbon and at sundry other Iberian ports in a dismal state. The events of Cádiz and Cape St. Vincent had severely interrupted Santa Cruz's mobilization plans, and all attempts to get back on schedule bogged down in general lethargy and mismanagement. Supplies were directed to the wrong stations, meat and biscuit moldered at one place while sailors at another place went hungry, cannon were left lying on quaysides because the required technicians could not be found to mount them on the ships. Furthermore, in early July, Santa Cruz was pulled from his harborside duties to chase after Drake. For weeks on end the marquis hunted about the Azores without success, and he did not return to Lisbon until September. His galleons, seaworn and weather-beaten, were in need of a thorough overhaul.

None of this swayed Philip from his intended purpose. The King's messengers galloped into Lisbon almost daily with directives to do this and that, prodding, pleading, ordering that the Enterprise of England take place immediately. The fleet must sail in October; if not then, it must leave in November. In December the fleet was still not ready, and Philip began to make biting accusations that his premier admiral was deliberately dragging his feet.

Santa Cruz had borne the full weight of the Armada preparations for almost a year, and Philip's thankless reproaches overlooked the fact that the old sea veteran represented the finest tradition of Spanish duty and achievement, and his country's best hope for victory. The Enterprise of England was largely his idea; it would have been the crowning glory of an illustrious career. It proved too much for him. He was now a tired 62. In the middle of January he took to his bed with fever and fatigue. By February 9, 1588, he was dead. The Armada seemed fated to remain forever in harbor.

To thwart raids on Spanish ports by privateers, an anonymous inventor dreamed up this gridlike underwater booby trap. Anchors would hold the grid two feet below the surface, and an unsuspecting enemy ship would first be holed by a series of swiveling spikes, then brought to a halt by rows of thornlike protuberances. Whether the Spanish ever built such a contraption is unknown.

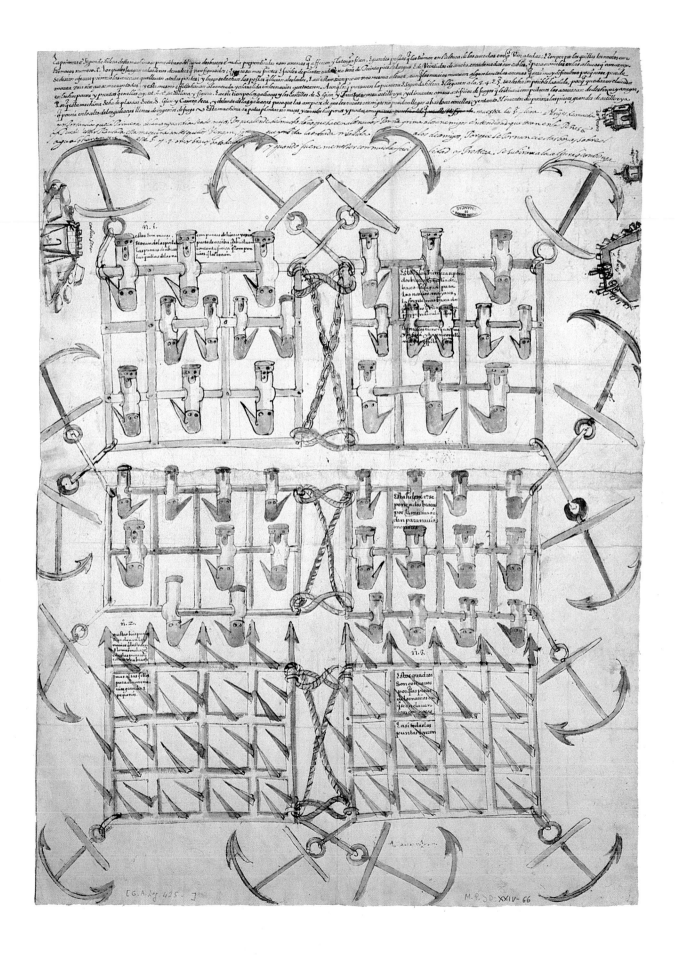

Chapter 3

"La Felicissima" sets sail

Improbably attired in scarlet court vestments by the 19th Century artist who created this scene, Lord Howard of Effingham visits Plymouth's waterfront to read the call to arms as England braces for the Spanish onslaught in 1588.

o astrologers and other seers of the period, 1588 was a year of dreadful portent. All manner of omens, from an alleged rain of blood in Sweden to a series of monstrous births in France, pointed to some earth-shaking catastrophe. Much of the foreboding harked back more than a century to the German astronomer Regiomontanus, author of the star tables used by Columbus and of a horoscope for the current year. According to Regiomontanus, there would be an eclipse of the sun in February, followed by two total eclipses of the moon. Saturn, Jupiter and Mars, harbingers of war and chaos, would linger in baleful conjunction in the moon's house. "If land and sea do not collapse in total ruin," Regiomontanus had concluded, "yet will the whole world suffer upheavals, empires will dwindle and from everywhere will be great lamentation." Students of numerology, sifting through the Bible, found reasons for alarm in the Book of Revelations and in selected passages from Isaiah. Events since the birth of Christ appeared to have moved in complex but predictable cycles, and the last cycle would conclude, with apocalyptic finality, in 1588. Surely the fall of some great kingdom was at hand.

As to the identity of the kingdom, there was lively speculation. Spain—Europe's only true empire—was a likely candidate for toppling, and nervous mariners throughout her possessions began deserting their ships in the ports where the Armada was assembling. To counter the mounting apprehension, King Philip ordered sermons denouncing all forms of wizardry and soothsaying. In England the omens seemed particularly worrisome; the second lunar eclipse, in August, would fall on the cusp of Virgo, Queen Elizabeth's birth sign. Like Philip, the English government tried to dispel the fears, issuing a pamphlet to refute the soothsayers. Catholics in France, presumably too full of Gallic *élan* to contemplate their own downfall, predicted Almighty punishment for the English Jezebel.

Whatever calamities the stars foretold, one prediction turned out to be dismally correct: 1588 brought the worst weather in memory. The Atlantic gales of December and January blew on into February and beyond, long past their season. Torrents of rain washed down on northern Europe, flooding croplands and turning roadways into knee-deep mud. A hailstorm in Normandy ravaged the orchards and, it was said, knocked cattle dead in their pastures. In Spain and Portugal, rains fell steadily. It was raining on February 9, as the Marquis of Santa Cruz lay dying at Lisbon. It was still raining three weeks later when the admiral's successor arrived to take command.

The Armada's new Captain General was Don Alonso Pérez de Guzmán el Bueno, the seventh Duke of Medina Sidonia. He was a country aristocrat of 38, short in stature, broad-shouldered, with brown hair and beard, and a melancholy countenance. His name was one of Spain's oldest, and his fortune was considerable: He owned orange groves in Andalusia and controlled the revenues of the local tuna industry. In his role as a provincial overlord, he was known for diligence and tact. But his talents as a military leader were largely untested; when Francis Drake had raided Cádiz harbor the year before, the Duke had hurried in with troops to defend the town—but the town had never come under attack. And nothing seemed to mark him for naval leadership. He had never captained a fleet of ships. He had never seen a battle at sea.

The last thing Medina Sidonia wanted was to conduct the Armada to England. While Santa Cruz still tossed with fever on his deathbed, Philip wrote Medina Sidonia a letter that hinted at the forthcoming command; the Duke's response was prompt and plaintive. "I wish I possessed the talents and strength necessary for such a great task," he wrote. "But, Sir, my health is too poor, for I know by my small experience afloat that I soon become seasick, and always catch cold. I am deeply in debt. My family owes 900,000 ducats, and I have not a single real to spend on the expedition."

Medina Sidonia's letter did no good, for Philip had made up his mind. "If you fail, you fail," the King wrote back, "but the cause being the cause of God, you will not fail. Take heart and sail as soon as possible." Undoubtedly the King placed special importance on Medina Sidonia's possession of a great name. In an age when ancestry counted for much, the Duke would command automatic respect from the proud and jealous sea captains at Lisbon. No lesser nobleman could quiet the squabbles over honor and precedence that were bound to develop after the death of the Marquis of Santa Cruz. And no doubt the King reasoned further that, despite his cries of poverty, the Duke would contribute handsomely to the Enterprise. In that the King would prove correct.

When Medina Sidonia arrived at the rain-swept anchorage at Lisbon in early March 1588, he found the fleet in a state of shocking dilapidation. No work had been done since Santa Cruz's death. A tumbled chaos of cargo and supplies littered the riverfront. Food and water were already turning foul; they were stowed in casks that had been hastily knocked together out of green wood—a legacy of Francis Drake's barrelburning during the previous year's blockade. Most of the men had been issued neither pay nor proper clothing. Worse yet, a typhus epidemic was raging through the ships. At a roll call of 22,000 troops, nearly 20 per cent were found to be sick, dead or missing.

Doggedly and methodically, Medina Sidonia set to work. He pored over battle plans and administrative files commandeered from Santa Cruz's private secretary. He began at once to untangle the general clutter of mismanagement and decay. Supplies were inventoried and distributed equitably among the ships. As the King had expected, Medina Sidonia personally contributed money to buy food and clothing and to meet the payroll. The ring of calkers' hammers again echoed through the dockyard as repair work and fitting-out resumed. At a time of individual glory-seeking and derring-do, the Duke was turning out to be a superb administrator.

One of his first tasks was to reorganize and strengthen the fleet's armament. Individual captains had been grabbing whatever they could in the way of guns and ammunition. Some ships were needlessly overarmed, others had guns without powder or shot, and still others were left with practically no weapons at all. Furthermore, reports from England gave a sobering estimate of the enemy's firepower. The Duke therefore assembled a council of sea captains and gunnery experts to advise him. At their suggestion he began redistributing artillery, transferring the

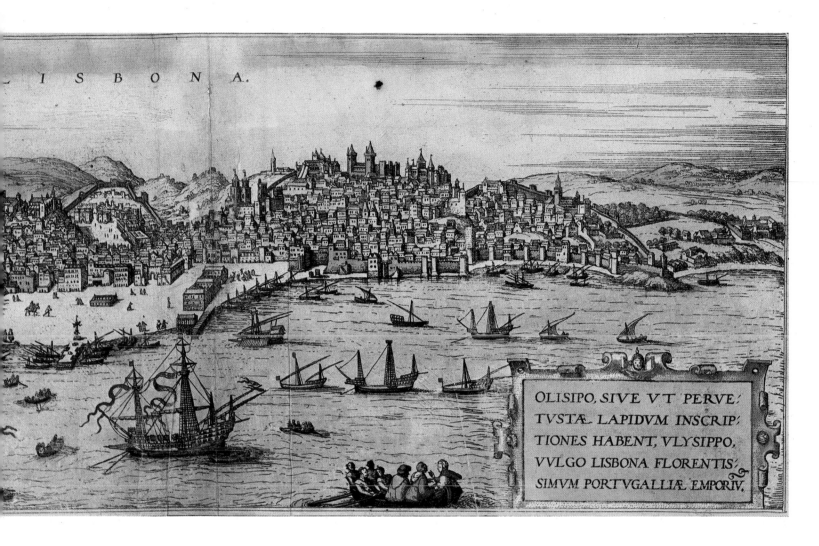

L I S B O N A.

OLISIPO, SIVE VT PERVE:
TVSTÆ LAPIDVM INSCRIP:
TIONES HABENT, VLYSIPPO,
VVLGO LISBONA FLORENTIS:
SIMVM PORTVGALLIÆ EMPORIV.

Almost every kind of craft that Spain could muster gathers in Lisbon harbor (above), the port of departure for the Spanish Armada. The mobilization lagged until the Duke of Medina Sidonia (left) assumed command; among other feats, he persuaded the arsenals of Madrid and Lisbon to turn out 66 new bronze cannon in just three months' time.

heaviest pieces to the frontline galleons and converted merchantmen. A frantic search took place for still more guns, particularly the heavy culverins and demiculverins that the English were known to be favoring. The Duke never found all the weapons he wanted, but he did manage to double powder allowances and to increase ammunition from 30 to 50 rounds of cannon shot per weapon.

At his advisers' behest, the new admiral undertook another, somewhat less enlightened, project. He proceeded to recarpenter some of his galleons and merchantmen, building up their lofty forecastles and sterncastles. This was directly contrary to the neat transformation that John Hawkins had made in Elizabeth's navy—cutting down top-hamper to render English ships more nimble and weatherly. Nonetheless, the Spanish captains loved their majestic castles, so perfectly suited to traditional tactics of grappling and boarding. Grapple and board was just what Medina Sidonia intended to do. The King himself had decreed as much, in his battle instructions to the fleet. How the Duke would bring his clumsy, towering ships alongside the fast and elusive English, no one bothered to explain.

Throughout the rainy spring, Philip bombarded the new commander in chief with a steady stream of counsel and encouragement, stressing

the need for haste. "The chief point is that the Armada should start," he told the Duke. To that he added countless other commands covering every last detail of the Enterprise of England. Make sure you find experienced pilots to guide you through the Channel, the King advised. Stay close to the English side, and so avoid the shoals and sandbanks along the French and Flemish coasts. Keep the fleet together; in case a storm should scatter it, name a rendezvous at Vigo, or Corunna on the Spanish coast, or, if the storm sends you that far, the Scilly Isles off England. Stay in constant touch with the Duke of Parma, and let him know your progress; send your messengers by sea to Dunkirk or Nieuport, or overland through Normandy. Avoid, if you possibly can, a pitched battle with Drake and the English fleet. Your task is to head for Cape Margate in the Thames estuary, to protect the landing of Parma's troops. You are not to land troops or undertake anything ashore at your own discretion.

The Duke was admonished in particular to cultivate the spiritual welfare of his fleet. "All victories are the gifts of God Almighty," the King wrote solemnly, "and the cause we champion is so exclusively His, we

At a 16th Century cannon foundry in the Low Countries, workmen (clockwise from the left) turn a treadmill, shovel scrap into the furnace, keep an eye on molten bronze as it flows into a mold, and chip away residue from cannon that have already been cast. The casting mold, submerged in the floor, stood vertically, breech end down. On the right, the artist has added a scene attesting to the power of the ordnance.

may fairly look for His aid and favor, unless by our sins we render ourselves unworthy." There must be no blasphemy in the fleet, no gambling, no petty arguing. No man should carry a dagger, everyone should confess his sins to a priest, and prayers should be sung twice daily. Above all, no wenching. This last order caused a considerable flurry when some 600 unidentified ladies were discovered keeping house in the ships. The Duke was scandalized. He had the women rounded up and expelled—not just from the fleet, but from Lisbon itself. The men complained bitterly, and were only partly appeased by the promise of pert and buxom lasses when they reached England.

Bit by bit, as the blustery March weather gave way to the gentler airs of April, the fleet grew in strength and readiness. By the end of Easter week, only a few last chores remained. After months of preparation and delay, it seemed that the departure would finally take place.

The fleet that assembled in Lisbon harbor was prodigiously strong, "the greatest navy that ever swam upon the sea," one observer declared. There were 130 vessels in all—58,000 tons of shipping, ranging from stately 1,000-ton galleons down to two- or three-masted *pataches* and tiny sloop-rigged *zabras*, the scouting and dispatch boats. Some 8,000 seamen had been conscripted to man the ships, which carried a polyglot fighting arm of more than 20,000 troops gathered from all corners of Catholic Europe. The Enterprise of England was to be a glorious crusade, crowning a century of Spanish triumphs over Saracen and Turk.

As befitted a crusade, 180 priests and friars signed up with the fleet to minister to the soldiers and mariners and to proselytize the English heretics. In case God's favor should lapse momentarily in battle, 85 surgeons and their aides were on hand to tend to the wounded. Looking toward the victory ahead, Philip had enrolled 19 justices and 50 administrators under an inspector general; they would set up a government of occupation in London. Quantities of gold traveled with them to finance the administration.

The ordnance that had been gathered seemed sufficient to batter down the strongest kingdom: 2,431 guns by one report, together with 123,790 cannon balls, 5,600 hundredweight of the best fine-grained musket powder and 1,200 hundredweight of match. For close-in fighting the fleet carried some 7,000 harquebuses, and 10,000 pikes and halberds. Beyond all this, a quantity of field guns had been trucked aboard for service ashore, together with 40 artillery mules and wagons, and all kinds of shovels, axes and other tools necessary for digging trenches and erecting siegeworks.

The ships' holds were crammed with provisions for six months—ton upon ton of rice, beans, fish, chick peas, bacon, biscuit, cheese, olive oil, vinegar. There were 147,000 pipes of wine and 12,000 pipes of reasonably fresh water. Each captain was issued a schedule of menus: six ounces of bacon per man on Sundays, six ounces of fish on Fridays and fast days, cheese on Wednesdays and Saturdays, and so on.

The Armada's 130 sail were grouped into 10 squadrons, according to their place of origin, with the principal fighting muscle falling into two frontline squadrons—the huge, powerful galleons of Portugal, and the somewhat smaller galleons of the Spanish province of Castile. The Portuguese ships, 12 in number, included the 48-gun, 1,000-ton *San Martín*, which Medina Sidonia took as his flagship. The Spanish group consisted of ten 500- to 700-ton galleons that normally were used as escorts for the Caribbean silver fleet, four large armed merchantmen from the Spanish Main and a few pinnaces. The commander of the squadron, a salt-bitten 20-year veteran of the West Indies trade named Don Diego Flores de Valdés, was known for his skill at map making and ship design—and for his foul temper. He constantly feuded with his fellow officers, who roundly disliked him. Nevertheless, Philip appointed him chief of staff under Medina Sidonia, and delegated to him the power of decision in matters of strategy, tactics and ship handling. Valdés sailed with the Duke, aboard the *San Martín*.

Four other vessels, strange hybrid craft known as galleasses, filled out the front line. Half sailing galleon and half oared galley, these vessels were impressive war machines of 50 guns each, "of such bignesse," said an English contemporary, "that they contained within them chambers, chapels, turrets, pulpits and other commodities of great houses." Each one also contained 300 hapless galley slaves, chained to benches. But the galleasses were fast and maneuverable, were able to operate in a calm, and could deliver a businesslike broadside. Great things were expected of them. The fleet also included four traditional galleys from Portugal for light-weather work.

The rest of the fighting craft, mostly armed merchantmen, were grouped into four squadrons of 10 ships each, and their commanders made up a roll call of Spanish naval gallantry.

Don Juan Martínez de Recalde, a battered campaigner of 62, led the Biscay ships. Brave, tenacious and fiercely proud, Recalde had been skippering fleets for 16 years. More than any other Armada officer, he was familiar with the seascape ahead; in 1580 he had conveyed the ill-fated battalion of papal volunteers to their landing on the southwest coast of Ireland (*page 18*).

The ships from Guipúzcoa, a province on the Bay of Biscay, sailed under the dashingly heroic Don Miguel de Oquendo, who had fought against the French in the Azores in 1582 and was nicknamed "Glory of the Fleet" for the fearless way he handled a ship. Another Azores veteran, Don Pedro de Valdés, commanded the 10 greatships from Andalusia; he was Diego Flores de Valdés' cousin and, it so happened, his bitter enemy—for reasons no longer known.

The fourth group of second-line warships, known as the Levant squadron, held a potpourri of vessels from ports friendly to Spain—Venice, Genoa, Barcelona and Naples on the Mediterranean, Ragusa (now Dubrovnic) on the Adriatic and Hamburg on the North Sea. The commander of that squadron, Don Martín de Bertendona, hailed from an old sea-faring line; his father had commanded the ship that carried Philip to England for his marriage to Mary. But the squadron's most glamorous fighter was a landsman—a brilliant young chevalier with blond beard and flaxen hair named Don Alonso de Leiva. He was designated to take command of the invasion should Medina Sidonia be disabled. He sailed in his own personal vessel, the 800-ton *Rata Santa María Encoronada*. With him went a spirited company of so-called gentlemen volunteers—

Spanish troops march across a 17th Century garden wall, commemorating epic naval struggles against the Turks at Lepanto, the French in the Azores and the English during the Armada campaign. The mural stands on an estate that once belonged to the Marquis of Santa Cruz, the great Spanish admiral who fought in the first two battles and directed the preparations for the Armada until his death in February 1588.

men of high birth and eager gallantry who had joined this crusade at their own expense, in quest of glory and renown, and had brought along retinues of squires and servants.

The last two squadrons of *La Felicissima Armada*—"The Most Happy Fleet," as it was called—were essentially noncombatant. They were a medley of pataches and zabras for picket and dispatch work, and a lumbering assortment of urcas heaped to near-bursting with extra provisions and equipment: spare gun carriages, horses and mules, the siege train, small arms and ammunition, oxhides for sealing up leaks, and other miscellaneous goods that included 8,000 leather flasks, 5,000 pairs of shoes and 11,000 pairs of sandals.

One crucial rite demanded observance before the fleet could sail. At 6 o'clock in the morning on April 25, a dazzling procession of warriors and dignitaries marched from the royal palace to the Cathedral of Lisbon. Across the high altar lay the enormous silk standard of *La Felicissima Armada*, resplendently embroidered by wives and mothers. The arms of Spain were shown flanked by life-sized figures of Christ crucified and the Virgin Mary, and into the fabric was worked an inscription in Latin: *"Exurge Domine et vindica causam tuam"* ("Arise, O Lord, and vindicate Thy cause"). Medina Sidonia knelt and grasped the standard's hem, while the Archbishop of Lisbon delivered a blessing. A volley of musket fire broke from the honor guard outside, and an echoing salvo thundered from the warships in the harbor. Then the entire company marched to the waterfront, where barges waited to ferry the voyagers out to the ships. It took two weeks to marshal the 29,000 men and remaining supplies on board. At length, on May 11, the lead ships began gliding downstream toward Belem, nearer the mouth of the Tagus, to await a fair wind for England.

The Armada's departure would come none too soon for the Duke of Parma, who had been marking time with his invasion troops in Flanders. Ever since the previous autumn, Parma had been pressing for the Enterprise to begin. In August he had captured the strategic city of Sluys, located at the head of a canal system linking his headquarters at Bruges with various key Channel ports. He had set thousands of workmen to widening and deepening the inland waterways to Nieuport and Dunkirk, the proposed sites of embarkation. For transporting his troops he had gathered a small flotilla of oared barges and canal boats. To these he had added some 70 pramlike craft with bow ramps for loading and discharging cavalry.

By September his army had reached peak strength of 30,000 Germans, Walloons, Spanish, Italians, Scots, even some renegade Englishmen— all of them disciplined soldiers. With a bit of luck—calm seas and a gentle easterly wind to push the flotilla along—this powerful troop could ease across the Flanders sandbanks on a high tide. In eight to 12 hours, if unmolested by Elizabeth's navy, it could reach the southeast coast of England. A few days' march would put it in London.

Armies are like prize fighters training for a bout: They reach a moment of supreme preparedness—muscles taut, reflexes swift, determination fixed at the highest pitch. But with a lull in activity they start growing flabby. This is what happened to Parma's invasion force. All through that dismal winter, as the snows and freezing rains held the battalions in camp, the war machine began to disintegrate. Provisions were consumed at an alarming rate—Parma had to send the cavalry inland to scavenge—and budgeted funds began to give out. As spring passed, the men went unpaid and unfed, and they began to sicken and to desert. "We are bound to conclude that the delay is for God's greater glory," Parma wrote in exasperation to Philip, "but the Enterprise, once so easy and safe, will now be infinitely more difficult, and will incur a much larger expenditure of blood and trouble."

Besides trying to keep an idle army in fighting trim, Parma faced some hard strategic realities. Nowhere along the Channel coast did he hold a really suitable deepwater embarkation port. English garrisons occupied Ostend, Dutch rebels held Flushing. The designated launch sites of Nieuport and Dunkirk were poor compromises, handicapped by mile after mile of shifting sand flats and thus inaccessible to all but the shallowest vessels. Worse yet, Parma was now being subjected to an increasingly heavy blockade by a squadron of Dutch flyboats based in Flushing. A flyboat was a fast, shallow-draft, two-masted gunboat of 140 tons or less, designed for just these waters. A pilot with good local knowledge could thread the channels between the sandbanks, and then blast the Duke's open-decked troop barges to kindling wood as they emerged from the harbor.

Parma was—mistakenly—relying on Medina Sidonia for extra help in the form of a detachment of pataches or zabras to hold off the flyboats

The Duke of Parma, Governor General of the Spanish Netherlands, wears the Order of the Golden Fleece, signified by the miniature ram that hangs at his chest. King Philip II awarded the Duke the honor for his siege of Antwerp in 1585. A complex man who combined military genius with a talent for diplomacy, Parma proceeded to govern the Netherlands —by his own account—"with a pardon in one hand and a sword in the other."

until he could reach full protection behind the main Armada squadrons. Beyond this he counted on surprising the enemy. He would lull the English into a false sense of security. To this end, all winter long, he sent delegates to Bourbourg, near the French border, to meet with emissaries from Queen Elizabeth in an elaborate charade of working out a peace treaty. Throughout the talks, Parma's representatives kept insisting that the build-up of troops in Flanders was for a local campaign. As for the frenzied activity at Lisbon, why that too was a local matter—an expedition to the Indies, or support for Catholic forces fighting Protestants in France. Certainly not an armada against England.

No one in England could possibly have been deceived. All Christendom buzzed with news of the Spanish preparations. Reports from the Continent flowed across the desk of Elizabeth's intelligence chief, Francis Walsingham. Medina Sidonia's full muster list of the fleet, detailing every last pinnace, cannon ball and wine cask, had been made public by the Council of War in Madrid, in the spirit of a boast. Protestant printers had seized upon this document and distributed it widely, adding their own suitably grim details. There would be a shipload of halters to hang all adult Englishmen, it was rumored. Irons were being loaded to brand heretic children on the cheek, scourges to whip women, and 3,000 to 4,000 wet nurses to suckle the bereaved infants. In the face of these reports, a peace treaty seemed unimaginable. "We might have peace," John Hawkins fumed, "but not with God. Rather than serve Baal, let us die a thousand deaths. Let us have open war with these Jesuits, and every man will contribute, fight, devise, or do for the liberty of our country."

The question was not whether the Armada would sail, but when, and England was ready. The country had been gearing up for it, on and off, for more than two years. Sharpened stakes had been driven into beaches along the southern coast. Entrenchments were dug, earthworks were heaped up as defenses against artillery fire. An elaborate network of signal towers was erected, with bonfires that could be touched off at the first sign of an enemy fleet. The blaze would be relayed from hilltop to hilltop, carrying the message along the coast and inland to every shire and hamlet. In London the renowned Italian engineer Federigo Giambelli was put to work improving defenses along the Thames. A set of drastic orders went out, to take effect should the Spaniards succeed in landing: Crops would be burned, cattle driven away, bridges demolished. And in town squares and village greens across the realm, ad hoc companies of militia began drilling: yeoman farmers and small tradesmen armed with pikes and muskets donated by the local squirearchy, and in some places with longbows, billhooks and harquebuses.

Never in memory had Englishmen joined together with such a burst of enthusiasm for a single cause. Even the nation's Catholics, whom Philip's advisers expected to rise in revolt, were putting patriotism ahead of religion and rallying wholeheartedly behind the Queen. "The battle will be bloody," predicted a diplomatic observer, "for the English never yield. They would count themselves victorious even if they died to a man along with the enemy, provided they could save the kingdom."

For all the patriotic fervor of the citizens, England's preparations went

Making ready for the onslaught

A set of 1587 engravings depict the London militia on parade. Musketeers take the lead, followed by fifers and drummers, then harquebusiers, pikemen

When word came that the Armada was on the way to invade England, the entire realm stood ready to throw the intruders out. Every important promontory on the coast had a warning beacon ready to light at the first sign of enemy sail. Every harbor susceptible to invasion had been mapped and fortified. Every county had a militia trained to march, to handle pikes and muskets, to understand various drumbeats—and had "thereby a courage put in them," as Queen Elizabeth's principal adviser, Lord Burghley, phrased it.

Any of at least a dozen ports was a possible target of the Spaniards. Yet regional claims of special peril and a need for extra-strong defenses were heard from every side. Sir Walter Raleigh insisted that Cornwall was in the greatest jeopardy of all: "There is no part of England so dangerously seated," he wrote, Cornwall "having the sea on both sides." Sir George Carey, a captain-general appointed by Queen Elizabeth, spoke out for Hampshire, saying: "No other shire of England hath a Portesmowthe and an Isle of Wighte therein to defende."

The Crown had its own ideas about the defense needs of the realm, and required every county to deliver a quota of men to the cause. It was surprised by some of the responses. Cornwall, for instance, came up with more than the required number of men to handle muskets and harquebuses, but not one of the 200 pikemen called for—a reflection of the growing faith in firepower's efficacy.

Inevitably, as the nation's apprehension mounted, there were false alarms. When a wisp of smoke rose near Portsmouth one afternoon, the local militia rushed to report for duty—only to find that some hunters had been trying to smoke a badger out of its hole.

Despite such mishaps, the defense plans of Elizabethan England were so well conceived that when Napoleon threatened another invasion 200 years later, essentially the same system of fortifications, beacons and county militias was reinstated.

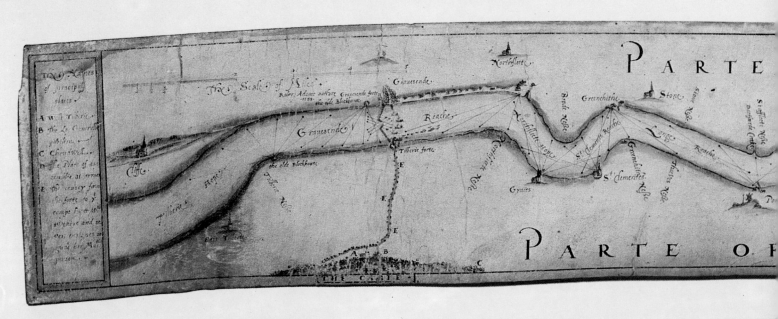

(trailing their weapons) and halberdiers. Pikes were 16 to 18 feet long and difficult to wield; only the strongest and nimblest men were trained to use them.

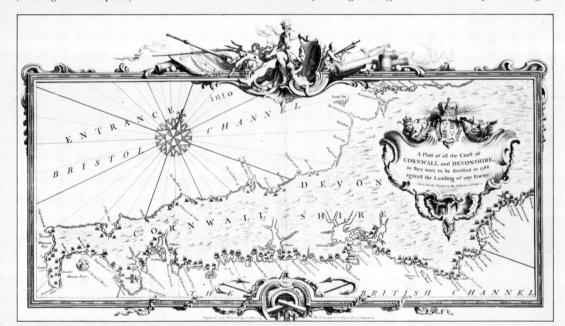

An engraving copied from a map made in 1588 shows how the coasts of Cornwall and Devon were to be defended "against the landing of any enemy." The haystack-like figures running eastward from Lands End past Exmouth represent bands ready to answer the call to arms.

This chart—oriented with north on the bottom—indicates the defenses of the Thames estuary from Tilbury upstream to London. The lines running diagonally from various sites on the riverbanks represent the fields of fire of nine strategically located gun batteries.

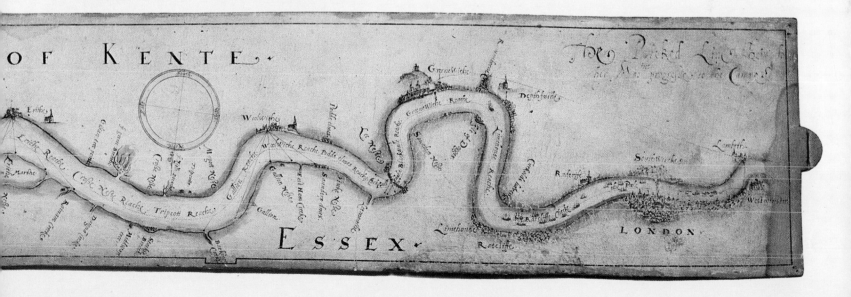

Warning beacons dot the Dorset coast and inland hills, ready to relay signals of the enemy's approach. Adjacent villages throughout the county took turns keeping watch, and each was required to post at least two guards by day, two by night.

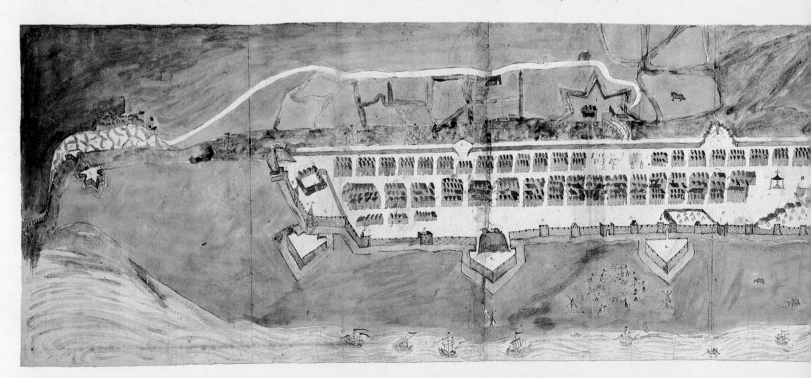

New walls, bulwarks, gun platforms, forts and a moat on the landward side of the town—all keyed to a list in the cartouche of this map—fortified Great Yarmouth on the North Sea. A force of 13,800 men stood ready to defend the port from the Spaniards.

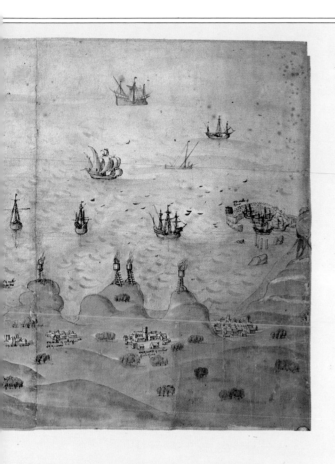

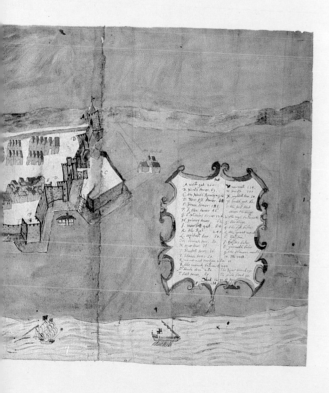

forward in an oddly haphazard way. There never seemed to be enough money, enough armaments, or sufficient direction from above. England kept no standing army, and the local militiamen tended to be a raffish lot. Some squads "have not been trained one day, so that they have benefited nothing, nor yet know their leaders," complained Sir Edward Stanley, who was in charge of the musters at Chester; "I want greatly powder, for there is little or none at all." Chester is in the north, near Liverpool, and was thus securely remote from attack. Matters stood more happily in the counties along the Channel. Somerset filled its muster "beyond expectation." Southampton assembled 12,000 men, though many of them, one official sniffed, were "rawly furnished, some whereof lacketh a headpiece, some a sword, some one thing or another that is evil, unfit or unbeseeming about him."

The one military arm that knew its business was the royal navy. John Hawkins' unflagging efforts on the Navy Board had given England the most effective seagoing force in its history: 18 frontline galleons ranging upward from 300 tons to the powerful 42-gun, 1,100-ton *Triumph*; seven smaller galleons in the 100- to 300-ton category; and several score of fast, trim pinnaces. A supplemental force of 22 armed merchantmen brought the fleet to 47 fighting sail—the speediest, sturdiest, best-armed warships in Europe. To this would be added any number of volunteer craft, manned and equipped at their owners' expense for the honor of defending the realm.

The greatest seafaring talents of the age had been placed in command. Sir Francis Drake was posted at Plymouth aboard the 450-ton *Revenge* with seven of the Queen's best galleons. Thomas Fenner, who had shipped with Drake to the Indies and to Cádiz, was vice admiral of the Plymouth squadron. Of other commanders in the squadron, Martin Frobisher, the stubborn and roughhewn hero of three expeditions in quest of the Northwest Passage, captained the *Triumph*, and Edward Fenton, a Frobisher protégé, was on the 600-ton *Mary Rose*. John Hawkins himself, at the Medway with the main fleet, commanded his reconditioned galleon, the 800-ton *Victory*. His son Richard was in proud command of the 360-ton *Swallow*. Sir William Wynter, hardened campaigner of 40 years' experience, veteran of the skirmish with the papal forces in Ireland in 1580, and onetime rival of Hawkins on the Navy Board, now plied the Dover Strait in the Hawkins-inspired *Vanguard*.

Only one commander had missed the trials and glories of a lifetime on the quarter-deck. He was Charles Lord Howard of Effingham, Lord High Admiral of England. But the post of Lord Admiral did not necessarily demand extensive shipboard experience. It dealt with lofty matters of policy and administration, and by custom was given to a top-ranking nobleman. Howard of Effingham qualified nicely in this respect. Peer of the realm, Knight of the Garter, first cousin to Queen Elizabeth, he claimed descent from one of the oldest families in England. He had never taken part in a battle at sea, but he was no stranger to naval affairs. His great-grandfather, his father and two uncles had occupied the post of Lord Admiral before him.

Howard had taken office in 1585, at the age of 50, and had plunged energetically to work. He had pushed Hawkins' efforts on the Queen's ships. He had smoothed the ruffled egos on the Navy Board. He had campaigned forcefully for more money, more ships, better food and conditions for seamen. Then, in December 1587, he took a commission for active sea duty. When the Armada appeared, he would sail to meet it as commander in chief of the English fleet.

The Queen had just acquired a fast new galleon, the 800-ton *Ark Royal*, built to Sir Walter Raleigh's order and donated to the navy in return for a £5,000 I.O.U. Howard placed his admiral's flag upon it. He was as delighted as a schoolboy with a Christmas toy. "I think her the one ship in the world for all conditions," he caroled to Lord Burghley, "and truly I think there can be no great ship make me change and go out of her." The grizzled peer then made an inspection tour of the other vessels in the Medway, crawling into bilges and forepeaks, prodding timbers for dry rot, testing the results of the royal dockyard's handiwork. "I have been aboard every ship that goeth out with me," he exclaimed, "and in every place where any may creep, and I do thank God that they be in the estate they be in; there is never a one of them that knows what a leak means."

The admiral's enthusiasm infected even the dour William Wynter.

Seamen clamber aloft to shake out the sails of the Ark Royal, the flagship in which Lord Howard led the English against the Armada. A four-masted galleon like the Ark Royal carried eight to 12 sails; to handle them required smart teamwork by no fewer than 270 mariners.

"Our ships doth show themselves like gallants here," Wynter declared. "I assure you it will do a man's heart good to behold them; and would to God the Prince of Parma were upon the seas with all his forces, and we in view of them!" Sir William was anxious to fight the Spaniards and beat them quickly, in time for his scheduled visit to Bath to take the waters.

Under Howard, a defense plan of sorts took shape. A squadron of 14 ships, led by Howard's cousin Lord Henry Seymour, and with Wynter as second-in-command, would continue patrolling the Dover Strait. The patrol unit could count on staunch assistance from the Dutch, who were maintaining an effective blockade of the Flemish coast. The main English fleet would sail west to join Drake at Plymouth. From there it would sail out to sea and wait in ambush for the moment when the Armada tried to enter the Channel. The supreme commander of this western fleet would of course be Howard. Drake would assume the role of Howard's vice admiral and principal adviser in matters of tactics and seamanship.

Drake was already in full command at Plymouth, and no one knew how cheerfully he would accept this new arrangement. England's first mariner was accustomed to giving orders, not taking them. There was some speculation that "a man born and grown up among freebooters would have found it irksome to practice the self-restraint admired by the ancient Romans," as one chronicler dryly phrased it. Nonetheless, when Howard put in at Plymouth at the beginning of June with some 40 galleons, merchantmen and auxiliaries, he pointedly carried with him a new vice admiral's flag for presentation to Drake.

As Lord Howard steered west to his rendezvous with Drake in the English Channel, the Spanish fleet under Medina Sidonia was belatedly nosing out from behind the cliffs that guard the mouth of the Tagus. No sooner had the Armada begun its stately progress downstream from Lisbon, almost three weeks before, than the foul weather of early spring had returned in force. A boisterous westerly gusted upriver, confining the ships to the harbor at Belem. There they waited for 18 tedious days. Not until May 29 did the wind moderate sufficiently, easing in force and veering into the north, to release the fleet.

At dawn on May 30, Medina Sidonia fired a single cannon blast, the signal to weigh anchor. A spirit of festive energy seized the ships: action at last. Answering trumpet calls brayed from 129 quarter-decks. Men sprang to capstans and yardarms, lines hummed in blocks, anchors broke through the water and the great sails dropped and filled to the breeze. A blaze of flags, pennants and banners cracked from more than 300 mastheads. Each squadron flew the colors of its region—the castles of Castile, the dragons and shields of Portugal, the cross and foxes of Biscay. The flagship San Martín displayed the giant standard that had been consecrated in the Lisbon cathedral, and the fleet's battle insignia, a red St. Andrew's cross on a snow-white field, streamed from the tip of her mizzenmast.

Sailing at last, the fleet made an astonishing spectacle. Its emblazoned spires were "trees of the faith" and "a jungle upon the sea," rhapsodized the poet Lope de Vega, who with his brother was embarked on this holy war against "the false Siren." And indeed, with its pomp and panoply, its glittering ranks of armed soldiers, its bejeweled cavaliers in their jauntily plumed casques, *La Felicissima Armada* seemed headed for certain victory. "The Invincible Fleet" was the name it went by in the taverns of Lisbon. Invincible, with God's good favor, all Spaniards believed it would surely be.

For two whole days the Armada glided down the Tagus, past the massive stone Tower of Belem, past robed prelates who stood on the heights to deliver a final blessing. By the evening of May 31, the last vessel had reached the open Atlantic.

Here the jubilant mood evaporated. As the fleet turned north toward England it found the wind blowing directly in its face. The same northerly breeze that had set it going now stopped it dead. The fleet had to work north in a zigzag progression of tacks. With each tack it lost ground to leeward. Many vessels, cranky and unwieldy under the best conditions, were so overloaded with soldiers and supplies, and so lacking in experienced mariners, that they could barely make headway. To keep the fleet together, Medina Sidonia had to order the faster galleons to reduce sail, "governing our progress," he lamented, "by the speed of the most miserable tub among us." In his second week at sea, the Duke had been pushed south as far as Cape St. Vincent.

A wind shift into the southwest sent the Armada back in the right direction, but by now other problems had arisen. The supplies of food and water, laded in at Lisbon more than a month earlier, were turning as foul as the weather had been. Cask after cask was opened and found to be unusable, its contents a green, putrid slime. Bacon, biscuit and cheese were heaved overboard in a state of advanced decomposition. An epidemic of dysentery raged through the ships. Two weeks after leaving Belem, the Armada had progressed scarcely 160 miles to Cape Finisterre; clearly it could sail no farther. On June 19, Medina Sidonia ordered the ships into Corunna, the handiest port, for reprovisioning.

As the sun fell, the *San Martín* hove into port, followed by some 50 of the faster ships. The slower vessels—the Levant merchantmen, most of the urcas, the Biscay squadron that was guarding them, the four galleasses and some small craft—were not so lucky. The evening was sultry, with ugly black clouds massing in the southwest, signs of a possible squall. Even so, the laggard vessels were told to stand outside the harbor until morning in order to make their anchorage in daylight. They were caught by the first gusts—not of a squall, but of the worst tempest of that dreary season. They were blown in all directions. Some went east into the Bay of Biscay. Others ran north before the gale. A few even fetched the Scilly Isles—about 450 miles away—and possibly Mounts Bay in Cornwall. Weeks went by before all the ships reassembled at Corunna, and by the time they did, several were dangerously battered, one was dismasted and the crews of all were sick and exhausted.

Medina Sidonia stayed a month at Corunna. "The men are out of spirit: the officers do not understand their business; we are no longer strong," he wrote the King. Nonetheless, the month was well spent. Several of the ships were fumigated, hauled and retallowed. Dock workers patched the damaged vessels. The ailing soldiers and crews limped off to the hospital. The water casks were cleaned and refilled, and fresh provisions were

ORDERS,
Set dovvne by the
Duke of Medina, Lord general
of the Kings Fleet, to be obſerued in
the voyage toward England.

Tranſlated out of Spaniſh into Engliſh by T.P.

Imprinted at London by Thomas Orwin for Thomas Gilbert, dwelling in Fleetſtreete neere to
the ſigne of the Caſtle. 1588.

Soon after the Armada left Lisbon, the instructions to the Spanish fleet—spelling out rules of behavior, rendezvous points, ration distribution and many other matters—were published in London in a booklet with this title page. How the orders reached England is not known, but the Spaniards made no secret of their mission: Similar translations appeared in other capital cities of Europe.

laded. A happier mood returned to the fleet. Near the end of the month, the Duke erected altars on an island in the harbor, and each man was marched up for absolution of his sins and Holy Communion. "This is great riches," the Duke proclaimed joyously; "they are now all well, content and cheerful." On Friday, July 22, *La Felicissima Armada* sallied forth once again for England.

For the moment the omens seemed favorable. The fleet glided north in a fair wind on a gentle sea. By the night of Monday, July 25, it had reached the Scilly Isles. Then, once again, the weather turned.

Tuesday dawned flat and overcast, with heavy showers and occasional gusts from the north. The gusts intensified during the night, backing into the west and bringing violent downpours. By Wednesday morning the seas were running so high they broke into the stern galleries of the warships. The four galleys, their timbers strained and their hulls all but swamped, had already fled toward France, the closest neutral land. There they would stay for the rest of the campaign.

The remainder of the fleet hove to under storm canvas while a full gale raged for 36 hours. It was Thursday morning before the skies cleared and the winds moderated. A momentary panic occurred when the *San Martín's* lookout counted more than 40 vessels missing, but all except one were later discovered hull down to leeward. The single loss was Recalde's flagship, the *Santa Ana*, which had staggered to shelter at Le Havre. Luckily for the Enterprise, Recalde himself had moved aboard the galleon *San Juan de Portugal*.

By Friday afternoon Medina Sidonia had regrouped his ships. He took sights and soundings to determine his position. The fleet had reached 50° N., the pilots said, with the lead touching at 56 fathoms. The readings indicated a position off Lizard Point, the entrance to the Channel: enemy waters. The sea seemed empty of life. Not a hostile sail could be seen. The horizon ahead lay as barren white as a field of glacial ice.

Moving into a tight battle formation, the fleet edged slowly forward under shortened sail. A hush fell over the men; they talked in whispers if they talked at all. About 4 p.m. an irregular blue line pushed above the wave crests on the horizon's edge. The fleet continued forward and, as the afternoon waned, the line rose higher and solidified into a shore front of gray-green hills and escarpments. Soon the lookouts noticed thin smudges of gray smoke rising from the land. In the gathering twilight, the smudges sharpened into pinpricks of light. The citizens of England had spied the Armada and had lighted the first signal fires along the coast of Cornwall.

To the mariners waiting at Plymouth, the spring gales that had so distressed the Spaniards brought only minor nuisance and frustration. The English commanders fought other problems that seemed to emanate from Her Majesty in London.

Lord Howard arrived off Plymouth on June 2, just three days after Medina Sidonia's departure from Belem. Drake had put out in full battle array to greet him, the Plymouth squadron of seven Queen's ships augmented by some 20 armed merchantmen and a flotilla of smaller craft. Salutes were fired, trumpets sounded, and Drake ceremoniously accepted his vice admiral's flag. The expected grumpiness of an old sea dog toward a desk admiral of noble birth simply never occurred. "I must not omit to let you know how lovingly and kindly Sir Francis Drake bearthe himself," Howard wrote Walsingham a few weeks later. By that time the Lord Admiral had become an outspoken convert to one of Drake's pet schemes: aggressive, long-range attack in Spain's home waters.

Ever since his triumph at Cádiz the year before, Drake had been pestering the authorities in London to let him repeat the insult. On March 30 he had composed a sharply worded message to the Privy Council: "With 50 sail of shipping we shall do more good upon their own coast, than a great many more will do here at home; and the sooner we are gone, the better." A few weeks later he had appealed directly to the Queen. "The advantage of time and place in all martial actions is half a victory; which being lost is irrecoverable," he wrote. "Wherefore if Your Majesty will command me away with those ships which are here already, and the rest to follow with all possible expedition, I hold it in my poor opinion to be the surest and the best course." Drake also unburdened himself of another gripe: scanty rations. "An Englishman, being far from his country," he wrote, "and seeing a present want of victuals to ensue, and perceiving no benefit to be looked for, but only blows, will hardly be brought to stay." But his main point came through loud and clear: Attack now!

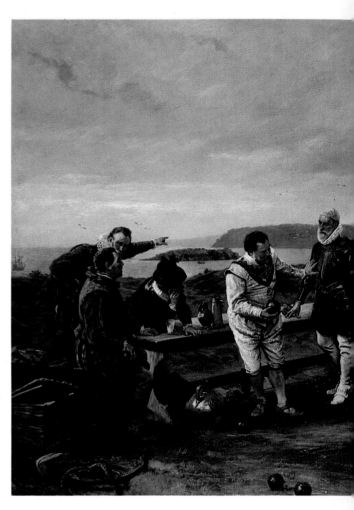

Queen Elizabeth had no intention of allowing her famous freebooter to go venturing abroad, or even of letting her fleet leave England. What if the Spaniards slipped past it undetected? And what if her peace delegates in Flanders suddenly reported success, just as Drake was assaulting Lisbon? She had sent Lord Howard to Plymouth with orders to "ply up and down" near the English coast, within easy call—and most likely with the secondary mission of cooling Drake's ardor. If this was her purpose, it backfired.

No sooner had the Lord Admiral set up headquarters than he began bombarding London with calls for immediate action and, like Drake, for more victuals. The need for food was urgent. While the Spaniards, who had stocked up for a six-month voyage, were heaving their polluted larders overboard, the English were meeting the spoilage problem by barely stocking at all. Meat was preserved on the hoof, bread as sacks of grain. This procedure would have been fine for a small squadron, but the combined fleet at Plymouth now numbered upward of 90 sail and some 10,000 men. Provisions, shipped from London in monthly allotments, were constantly being delayed in the Channel by contrary winds. "There is here the gallantest company of captains, soldiers and mariners that ever was seen in England," Howard wrote Lord Burghley; "It were pity they should lack meat when they are so desirous to spend their lives in Her Majesty's service." Even so, short-rationed as he was, Howard was determined to set sail. "God send us a wind to put us out, for go we will, though we starve," he declared. If provisions gave out, no matter. There were plenty of fish in the sea.

As Howard and Drake waited fretfully at Plymouth, reports from Spain showed that the Armada had already left Lisbon, that it had met a severe storm, and that it was now piecing itself back together at Corunna. Even Elizabeth saw the advantage of striking while the enemy was

Sir Francis Drake and Lord Admiral Howard casually play a game of bowls on a grassy hill overlooking Plymouth Sound as a smoke beacon behind them signals the sighting of the Armada to the next town up the coast. Though the bowling game may be legendary, it reflects the serene self-assurance with which the English met their foe—and a more prosaic fact as well; they had a seven-hour wait for an ebb tide before their ships could leave the harbor.

down. A messenger sped into Plymouth with royal permission for the fleet to embark when ready.

In high jubilation, the Lord Admiral led his ships out of harbor and trimmed his sails for Corunna—only to meet the same kind of ill luck that had been dogging the Spaniards. He was turned back by head winds. He tried again a few days later, with the same sad result. Four times the English steered south for Spain, and four times they were baffled by the weather. The last attempt took them halfway down the Bay of Biscay, until they could all but glimpse the Galician sierra. But again the breeze hauled into the south. To try beating against it, with rations almost exhausted, would have been a form of slow suicide. Howard swung about and rode the southerly home, dropping anchor in Plymouth on Friday, July 22. It was the same day that Medina Sidonia, embarking at Corunna, had set his helm toward England.

The gale that had caught the Spaniards at the Channel entrance found the English comfortably sheltered in Plymouth. To John Hawkins and his countrymen, riding at anchor in the 800-ton *Victory*, the storm was no more than "a little flaw." The English spent the week restocking their ships, replacing worn spars and rigging, and plugging some leaks that had opened up during the last trip south. Some of the men had come down with fever, and they had to be replaced by fresh recruits. Morale continued high nonetheless. "There shall be neither sickness nor death which shall make us yield until this service be ended," Howard declared. The same resolve burned in the heart of every man in the fleet.

Events at Plymouth now slide briefly from history into legend. After a midday meal on Friday, July 29, so the story goes, Howard and Drake took time from their labors to climb up Plymouth Hoe, a grassy promontory overlooking the outer harbor, and indulge in a game of bowls. Sometime around 3 o'clock, Captain Thomas Fleming of the bark *Golden Hind* came dashing up the Hoe with a singular piece of intelligence. Fleming was assigned to picket duty at the Channel entrance, and that morning he had sighted an enormous cluster of enemy warships. They were gathered on the horizon off the Lizard in southwest Cornwall, and they appeared to be standing by with sails struck, as though waiting for something. (They were waiting, in fact, for the vessels that had been blown to leeward in the storm.) Fleming was a reasonably seasoned mariner, but the sight of these ships gave him an adrenalized shudder. With their gaudily painted topsides, their streaming banners, their castellated towers, they made the mightiest congregation of fighting sail he had ever seen. The Armada had arrived.

Fleming's news caught the English in an awkward position. A southwest breeze was whipping into Plymouth Sound, along with an incoming tide. For the moment the fleet was locked in harbor. If the Spaniards were to bear down on a fair wind and attack now, little could be done to resist them. Even so, the two English commanders reacted with easy aplomb. The first words spoken, the legend says, were Drake's: "We have enough time to finish the game and beat the Spaniards, too."

That said, the two calmly continued to roll their bowling balls across the green at the Hoe. As the tide turned fair at evening, they walked down to dockside to guide their ships out to sea for the coming battle.

82

A multifarious fleet for Philip's crusade

With its looming, castellated stern gallery and strongly planked hull, the three-masted galleon—the major battleship of the Armada—displaced from 250 to 1,000 tons. The largest galleons mounted up to 50 heavy ship-killing guns and carried 500 sailors and soldiers.

"To see them under sail is to witness the splendor of a city-like multitude of the greatest ships of the world." So exclaimed a Spaniard who journeyed to Lisbon to watch the departure of the Armada. Indeed, the fleet's 130 ships were a spectacularly diverse collection that embodied maritime traditions of Spanish-held lands bordering the Mediterranean, Adriatic and Baltic Seas, as well as the Atlantic itself.

The principal burden of fighting for the Spanish cause fell to 20 galleons. These vessels generally reflected con-

temporary warship design, but their castles were higher than those of the English ships. Strongly constructed and heavily armed, the galleons had long served at the perilous work of escorting treasure convoys across thousands of miles of ocean, and they were expected now to match any vessel the enemy might possess.

Supplementing the galleons were eight warships from various Mediterranean locales. Half of them were galleys, whose low-slung design and dual modes of propulsion—by oars and a

GALLEON

lateen rig—had evolved during the early days of Mediterranean seafaring. Kin to these sleek craft were four massive square-rigged galleasses, hybrids born of the desire to unite the seaworthiness and armament of the contemporary galleon with the maneuverability of the ancient galley.

The battle force was filled out with 44 carracks, merchantmen commandeered from all over the Empire. To meet the demands of war, they were given extra armament and lofty superstructures for close combat.

Providing support for the fighting ships were other miscellaneous vessels that also had been recruited from Philip II's seaports. Included among them were nearly two dozen small pataches—vessels that normally served for coastal patrol duty—and a flotilla of 23 urcas, ships capacious enough to transport bulky cargoes of lumber from the Baltic Sea to ports around Philip II's dominions; now they would freight to England the stores and provisions that were to sustain the mighty Spanish force in the fight ahead.

The large, shallow-draft, oar-equipped galleass measured more than 150 feet from its iron-tipped battering ram to its stern and carried 50 guns. Although awesome in appearance, the galleass was too cumbersome to outmaneuver galleons.

GALLEASS

84

The graceful galley, well suited for sheltered Mediterranean waters and for hand-to-hand combat afloat, was looked upon by the Spanish commanders as a marginal addition to the Armada. The lateen rigging and shallow draft made her too frail for northern winds and seas.

A nimble sailer, the 70-ton patache handled a bigger assignment than her diminutive size would suggest. She scouted ahead, carried orders from ship to ship and delivered dispatches from the fleet to the shore. In battle, pataches gathered together to screen the lightly armed supply hulks from enemy assault.

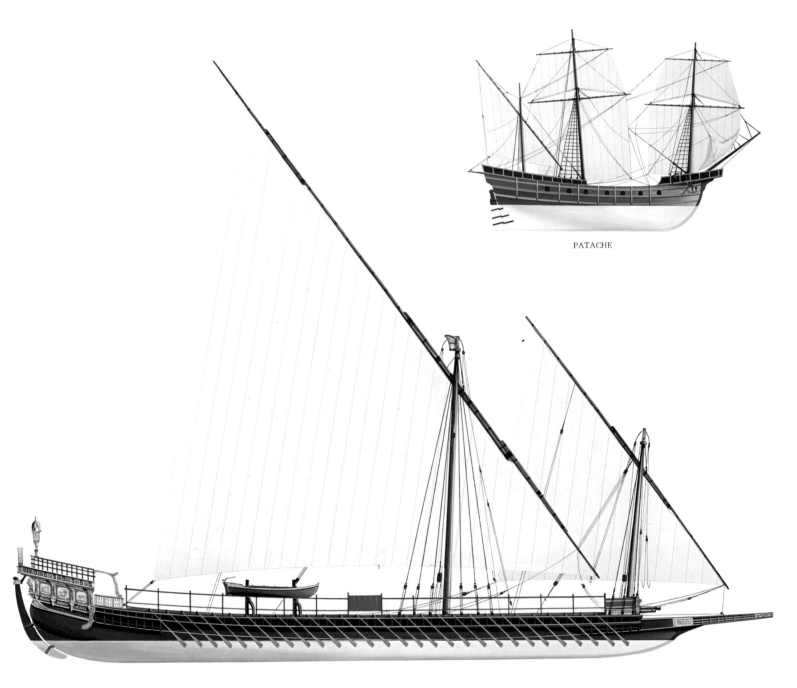

PATACHE

GALLEY

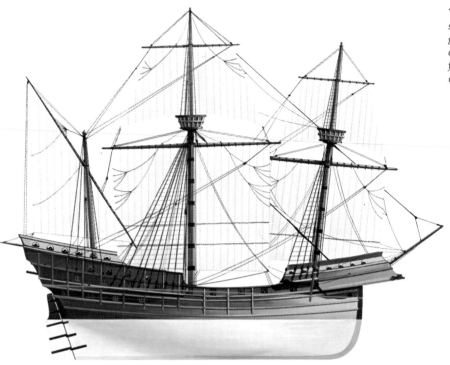

The square-rigged carrack, though slower and not so sturdy as the Spanish galleon, could hold her own in battle after being armed with heavy artillery and fitted out with high bow and stern castles meant for fighting at close quarters.

CARRACK

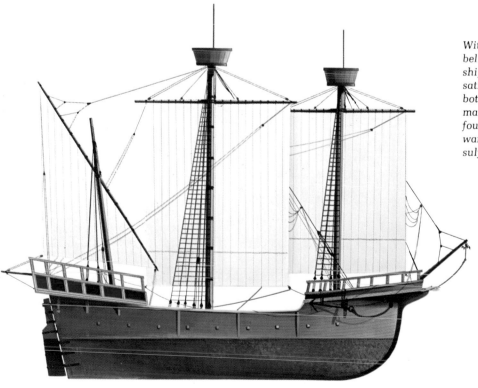

With a plain three-sail rig and a wide-bellied hull, the urca was the clumsiest ship in the Armada—but entirely satisfactory as a transport. The dark-hued bottom of the hull resulted from Baltic mariners' use of pitch and tar to prevent fouling; by contrast, the coating on warm-water ships was a mixture of tallow, sulfur, crushed glass and white lead.

URCA

Chapter 4

Gun smoke in the Channel

or a full 24 hours after sighting the Cornish coast on the afternoon of Friday, July 29, the Armada crept slowly eastward up the Channel without catching a glimpse of the English fleet. A light breeze drifted in from the west-southwest, the Spanish warships ghosting before it in a platinum haze, the gray-green hills of Cornwall rising and fading to port behind a thin surface mist. The most heavily gunned fleet in history was stalking its prey with eerie and circumspect quiet.

Medina Sidonia spent Saturday morning conferring with his captains, writing dispatches, and brooding over the uncertainties ahead. A site for the rendezvous with the invasion troops at Dunkirk still had to be established. Although the admiral had prodded the Duke of Parma with almost daily inquiries, there had been no reply. Not a syllable of instruction, not a breath of acknowledgment. "I am astonished to have received no news of him for so long," the admiral complained in a handwritten postscript to a dispatch to the King; "we are consequently groping in the dark." And where were the English? When would they show themselves? At one point a lone enemy pinnace had darted up, seemingly from nowhere, and then skipped off to the indignant rattle of Spanish guns. It was the only evidence, other than the signal fires on shore, of the English presence. The Armada slipped eastward through the mist, toward an unseen enemy and an unspecified appointment with its silent ally in Flanders.

A slight stir of excitement broke the hush around four in the afternoon. The fleet drew into a shallow scallop of coastline in the lee of a slate-gray headland (Dodman Point, most probably, about halfway between the Armada's landfall at the Lizard and the English base at Plymouth). As the ships rounded up to assess their position, the lookouts called down from the mast tops. Far to the east, some 15 miles ahead, they had spotted the glint of sunlight against canvas. The lookouts tried to count the sails, but a cloud passed over the sun, and then a curtain of sudden rain obliterated the sight. That was all.

Just whose ships they were, and how many, the Spaniards could only guess. Most likely they belonged to Francis Drake, who was known from previous intelligence reports to be stationed at Plymouth with a small squadron. Earlier that day, at a war council aboard the *San Martín*, someone had proposed that the Armada make an immediate attack on Plymouth, gambling on surprise to catch and sink Drake's squadron at its moorings. The proposal evoked a heated discussion that only a forceful command from Medina Sidonia could silence; he insisted that the fleet follow its sailing orders, which were to continue upchannel for the rendezvous with Parma. If Drake insisted on gunfire, he would get it; but the King himself had cautioned that it would be foolhardy to tangle with

With royal streamers rippling in the wind, the Spanish Armada (flying scarlet flags emblazoned with gold) and the English fleet (wearing white flags with the red cross of St. George) converge in the English Channel in 1588.

Drake unnecessarily. In any event, if the ships that had just been sighted belonged to Drake's squadron, a surprise attack on Plymouth was out of the question. The Duke sent a pinnace through the gathering dusk to reconnoiter. While awaiting its return, he ordered his captains to tighten the fleet's battle formation.

The placement of the squadrons had been worked out at Lisbon months before, with all the detailed precision normally given to drilling troops on a parade ground. The principal fighting ships were deployed in three major divisions: a vanguard led by Don Alonzo de Leiva and Martín de Bertendona of the Levant squadron; a main battle group centered on the galleons of Portugal and Castile, with Medina Sidonia in tactical control; and a rear guard under Juan Martínez de Recalde and his Biscay squadron. The noncombatants—supply urcas and dispatch boats—were tucked neatly in the middle, between the main battle group and the Biscayans. The ships were ranged flank to flank, six or seven miles apart, in a variation on standard line abreast; instead of forming a straight line, the ships took on the shape of a crescent moon. The arc pointed upchannel; the center was thickened with the urcas, and the horns trailed to windward with various elements of the rear guard.

A portion of a letter written to the Grand Duke of Tuscany by his ambassador at Lisbon on May 18, 1588, reveals a sailing plan for the Armada, complete with the names of the ships' captains (numbered 1 through 15) and the positions the ships would take (in squadrons designated by letters). The Spanish Crown had commandeered the Duke's prize galleon (No. 14) for the great endeavor.

Sometime after midnight, the reconnaissance pinnace returned from patrol—with four captive English fishermen and some important information. The fishermen had come that day from Plymouth, where they had watched the English ships being towed out of harbor—not only Drake and his squadron, they said, but the main force of the English fleet under the command of Lord Admiral Howard. This was worrisome news. Until now, the Spanish commanders had assumed that Howard was at the far end of the Channel, 250 miles to the east, guarding the Dover Strait. Now it seemed that the Armada was about to confront the full combined might of English sea power.

There was nothing to be done about it yet, however, and so the Armada continued to drift eastward under shortened sail. The wind was still astern, but during the night it began to veer toward west-northwest, blowing the sky free of clouds and uncovering a quarter moon. At about 2 o'clock in the morning another phantom glimpse of the English appeared in the thin, silvery light.

Near the shore, in the direction of Plymouth, stood a small detachment of warships. Like the ships sighted earlier, they were well to the east and thus safely to leeward. To Medina Sidonia and his officers it seemed that, when the battle was joined, the Armada would enjoy the commanding advantage of the weather gauge. But as the night wore on, the lookouts reported that the ships were inching to windward along the coast in a series of short tacks. By Sunday morning the detachment had come abreast of the Spanish fleet—and as the sun rose on a sparkling sea, another cry rang down from the mast tops. A great fleet of ships, as many as 80 sail, the lookouts reported, could be seen in the southwest, bearing down on the Armada's rear—and with the wind astern. Before a shot had been fired, the first crucial battle maneuver had been won by the English. They had captured the weather gauge.

From the moment Captain Fleming had raced up Plymouth Hoe to report the Armada's arrival on Friday afternoon, Lord Howard had felt no uncertainty about what to do. He would lead the fleet to sea, away from Plymouth, in order to gain the windward position. This plan took considerable daring, since it would leave the port virtually unprotected, but the tactical advantage of the weather gauge was deemed worth the risk. By 10 o'clock that evening Howard and his captains were moving the ships away from their moorings on the ebb tide.

Launching the fleet was tricky, laborious work. A stiff wind blew directly into the harbor, causing "great trouble and difficultie," a chronicler noted. Each ship had to be either towed into Plymouth Sound behind rowboats or hauled along by cables run out from shore. The Lord Admiral bustled about the docks, barking orders and words of encouragement, from time to time grabbing and hauling on the cables himself. Once clear of the harbor, the ships began beating out to sea. By noon on Saturday, Howard had boarded the flagship *Ark Royal* and had led 54 sail as far as the Eddystone, a cluster of rocks nine miles to the south of Plymouth. A few hours later the sky cleared, briefly revealing the Spanish fleet hull down in the west. As the weather closed in again, Howard continued moving in long tacks to the southwest, skirting the Armada's seaward wing. By the early-morning hours of Sunday, July 31, he had rounded up behind the Spanish rear, where the Spanish lookouts would discover him at daylight.

To the English, the full view of the Spanish fleet against the sunrise was awesome. "You could hardly see the sea," exclaimed one observer, so thick was the gaudy clutter of masts, sails, banners and battlements. Another described the sight with rhapsodic wonder: "the Spanish fleet with lofty Turrets like Castles, in Front like a Half-moon, the Wings thereof spreading out about the length of seven Miles, sailing very slowly, though with full Sails, the Winds being as it were tired of carrying them, and the Ocean groaning under the weight of them." While the English looked on, the enemy fleet edged in toward Plymouth, as though preparing to attack the port. At the same time it began adjusting its battle order, bringing some of the ponderous galleasses to the rear to meet the expected assault from Howard.

The English captains had never seen anything like the slow, martial precision with which the towering Spanish ships moved into place. Their own experience was limited to buccaneering raids and encounters with small squadrons, and they had never thought to develop unified tactics for an entire fleet. Now, as they watched, the Spanish performance evoked a grudging admiration—and not a little perplexity. How to meet the maneuver? An attack on the center would invite disaster; the two wings would close in and envelop the attacking vessels like the jaws of a shark. The wing tips themselves were guarded by some of the fleet's most powerful galleons, but the formation was looser there. At the wings, then, the attempt must be made.

The two fleets edged closer, both wary. By 9 a.m. on Sunday they faced each other off Plymouth, and the hour had come for battle to open. It did so with exquisite courtliness, in a gesture of high chivalry. Medina Sidonia unfurled the royal standard from his foretop—the signal to engage—and Lord Howard, flinging a gauntlet in the face of imperial Spain, dispatched his personal pinnace, the *Disdain*, "to give the Duke of Medina defiance." The *Disdain* unloaded a solitary culverin shot in the direction of the Spanish flagship, then scurried back upwind to rejoin the English fleet.

The challenge given, Howard led his principal galleons in single file past the Armada's southern wing. Guns blazing, he bore down on the large vessel stationed at the wing tip, which he assumed to be the Spanish flagship. It was, in fact, a ship from the Levant squadron, most probably the 800-ton carrack *Rata Santa María Encoronada*, carrying Alonso de Leiva and his gentlemen volunteers. Howard's *Ark Royal* and Leiva's *Rata* swung north, broadside to broadside, and steered along the rear of the Armada crescent toward the opposite end, the landward wing. Howard kept a distance of some 400 yards between the two ships—just close enough for his master gunners to graze the *Rata*, and just too far away for the less expert Spaniards to hit back.

The rest of the Levant squadron turned north behind the *Rata*: Martín de Bertendona's huge carrack, the 1,200-ton *Regazona*, the Armada's largest vessel, and eight other heavy warships. They represented an extraordinarily powerful force—more than 8,000 tons of shipping, 280 guns and some 2,800 gunners, pikemen, harquebusiers and swordsmen itching to grapple and board the English. But they could not come close. Try as they might, the hulking Levanters simply could not sail high enough into the wind to narrow the corridor of water between the two groups of ships. Howard, with his fast, close-winded galleons pecking away with long shots, never gave them a chance.

While Howard worked north, keeping the Spaniards at a gingerly arm's length, a second action erupted at the Armada's landward wing. A line of English ships, led by Drake in the *Revenge* and including John Hawkins in the *Victory* and Martin Frobisher in the 1,100-ton *Triumph*, charged down on the weathermost Spanish vessel. This was the 1,000-ton galleon *San Juan de Portugal*, flagship of the Biscay squadron, commanded by Juan Martínez de Recalde. She bristled with 50 guns and some 500 fighting men.

The rest of the Biscay squadron continued downwind with the main

This engraving—one of a series commissioned by Lord Admiral Howard—charts the early phases of the Channel fighting. English ships emerge from Plymouth harbor (1) and mass behind the Spaniards' crescent before attacking its northern wing (2). Later, the two fleets disengage, and the English pursue the Spaniards—now fallen out of crescent formation—up the Channel (3).

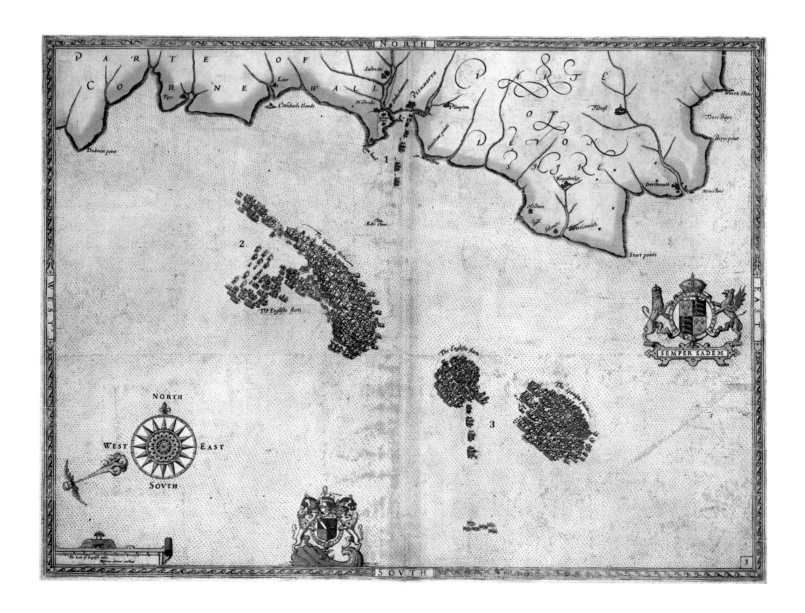

fleet, but Recalde turned the *San Juan de Portugal* to face the English onslaught alone. The gambit was extraordinary, an apparently inexcusable fracturing of the Armada's disciplined battle order, and no one knows exactly why it occurred. Perhaps there had been a mix-up of signals among the Biscayans. It is more likely, however, that Recalde, in a rush of pugnacious gallantry, was setting himself up as bait, deliberately provoking Drake to sail in close. He may have hoped that he could force an opportunity to hurl his grappling lines or perhaps that he might spark a general melee between the two fleets.

To Drake, the prospect of grappling and boarding the lone Spanish galleon must have seemed an almost irresistible temptation, but he refused it. Instead he stood off at a distance of 300 or 400 yards, and for the next two hours the *Revenge*, the *Victory* and the *Triumph* battered the *San Juan de Portugal* with culverin and cannon fire. During that time the thundering cluster drifted downwind, and gradually a number of frontline Spanish ships drew up to help defend Recalde. The *Gran Grin* came about, along with some of the other Biscay vessels. The *San Martín* and another vessel, the Portuguese *San Mateo*, luffed up with topsails struck and sheets flogging, an invitation to close combat. The *Rata*, which by now had sailed the length of the Armada crescent, from the southern wing to the northern one, tried to engage the *Revenge*. It seemed that a melee might indeed occur.

The English never let it happen. With the arrival of the rescue ships, Howard hoisted the signal to disengage. As Drake and his squadron worked back upwind to rejoin the main fleet, the Spaniards attempted to follow. The stately vessels, heeling gently, their yards braced in hard, tacked back and forth in an effort to recover the wind, but the English always glided out of reach. By midafternoon the Spanish quit trying. The battle of Plymouth was over.

It had been more of a skirmish than a real battle, the first in a series of hit-and-run artillery duels that would attend the Armada's advance up the Channel and on toward Dunkirk. The two fleets had sniffed at each other like a pair of powerful mastiffs, snapping and growling at the ends of their leashes, without ever coming to serious blows. Neither side had taken much punishment. Not a single English vessel was reported hurt, and the Spaniards had sustained only minor damage. The *San Juan de Portugal's* forestay had been shot away, two great iron balls had lodged in her foremast, and perhaps a dozen men had been critically wounded. No more than that.

Both sides had found the brief encounter frustratingly inconclusive. Aboard the *Ark Royal*, Lord Howard gathered his captains to a conference, then composed a brief report to Walsingham. "I will not trouble you with any long letter," he wrote; "we are at this present otherwise occupied than in writing." In a plea for ammunition, he added: "For the love of God and our country, let us have with some speed some great shot sent us of all bigness; for this service will continue long." Howard's vice admiral concurred. "They are determined to sell their lives with blows," Drake exclaimed.

The English saw no hope, in fact, of gaining a quick and satisfying

Juan Martínez de Recalde, vice admiral of the Spanish fleet, was an experienced mariner who had fought in battles all over the world—against the Portuguese in India, the English in Ireland, the French in the Azores. The fighting mettle of the English greatly impressed him, and he reportedly said that a successful invasion by the Armada would be a "miracle" —albeit one he fully expected to occur.

victory. The Armada appeared to be so strong, its battle array so disciplined and invulnerable, that, Howard confessed, "we durst not adventure to put in among them." The admiral could see that his guns, though they had "thundered thick and furiously," were having little effect; not a single round had been observed to penetrate a Spanish hull. The English ordnance simply did not carry enough punch at the distances at which Howard was choosing to fight. But if the English moved in closer, they would expose themselves to a ship-smashing barrage of heavy cannon, demicannon and perrier fire, and to a suicidal risk of being boarded and captured. Howard saw only one course: to tail the Armada as it glided up the Channel, nipping at its wings as the opportunity arose.

Besides his tactical problems, Howard faced a serious strategic threat. The Spaniards had already slid past Plymouth, but a real danger existed that they would try to make a landing nearby, at Tor Bay or upchannel at the Isle of Wight. Both possibilities had to be thoroughly erased. As the daylight faded, Howard put Drake in the lead and gave the popular hero the honor of guiding the fleet, a role that Howard might have been expected to undertake himself.

Medina Sidonia was scarcely more pleased with the day's action than Howard. The English seemed to have no stomach for fighting—at least not for fighting the way the Duke imagined it, with swordplay and musket fire and ships bound together in a snare of grappling lines. Having lost the weather gauge and the initiative, he saw no way to bring on such an encounter. "Their ships are so fast and nimble," he noted with dismay, "they can do as they like with them."

As his vessels returned to their places in the Armada crescent after the fighting, two new problems arose. One seemed inconsequential—at first. The flagship of the Andalusian squadron, Pedro de Valdés' 1,100-ton carrack, the *Nuestra Señora del Rosario*, snapped off her bowsprit in a collision with another vessel of her own squadron. The damage was minor and easily repaired. The other problem was more serious. Around 4 p.m. a thunderous burst of fire and smoke erupted from the center of the fleet. The 900-ton *San Salvador*, the almiranta of the Guipúzcoa squadron, had blown up.

No one knows just how it happened. Perhaps a gunner had been careless while cleaning the smoldering wadding out of his weapon, and had dropped sparks on a nearby powder cartridge. Perhaps it was sabotage. One story has it that the ship's ordnance master, rebuked for smoking on the quarter-deck, had defiantly knocked the ashes of his pipe into a powder keg. By another account the culprit was an impressed Fleming who had somehow managed to ship his wife aboard; a Spanish infantry captain, claiming *droit du seigneur*, had taken the wife to bed, and the husband in cold fury had laid a trail of powder to the magazine, ignited it and leaped overboard.

Whatever the cause, the effect was catastrophic. The gunpowder stored in the afterhold had exploded, catapulting the poop and the sterncastle into the sky and killing more than 200 men. Hearing the explosion, Medina Sidonia fired a cannon to halt the fleet and turned back to assist; finding the *San Salvador* ablaze, he ordered her bow turned into

The nascent art of seagoing gunnery

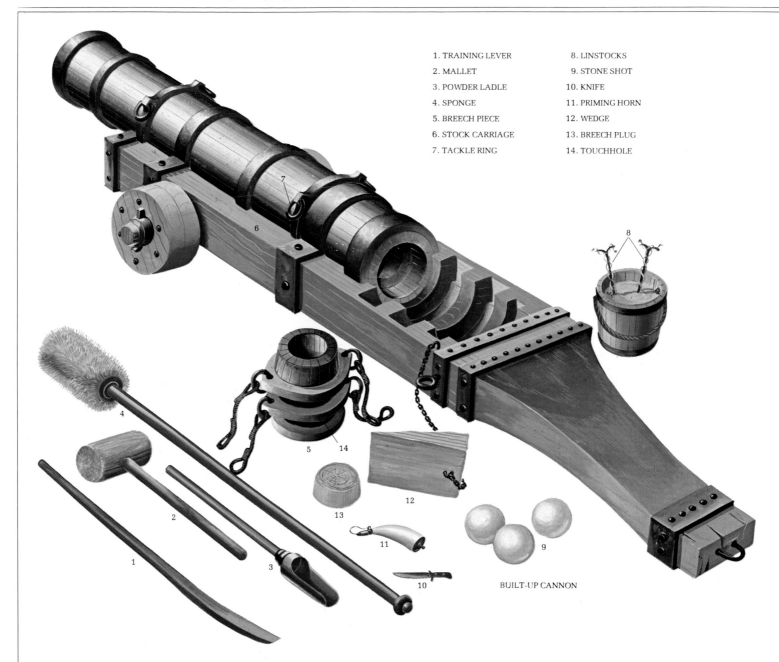

1. TRAINING LEVER
2. MALLET
3. POWDER LADLE
4. SPONGE
5. BREECH PIECE
6. STOCK CARRIAGE
7. TACKLE RING
8. LINSTOCKS
9. STONE SHOT
10. KNIFE
11. PRIMING HORN
12. WEDGE
13. BREECH PLUG
14. TOUCHHOLE

BUILT-UP CANNON

When the English and the Spaniards clashed in 1588, each side had more than 20 sorts of ship-mauling cannon. They ranged in size from five-foot guns weighing about 1,200 pounds to 14-foot behemoths whose weight exceeded four tons. Some threw balls of stone, others balls of iron.

For all that variety in detail, the cannon fell into two categories, exemplified by the weapons pictured here. One type was built up of wrought-iron staves and hoops that were welded together and then fitted with a detachable powder chamber. The other type was made in a single piece by casting bronze in a clay mold. These construction differences were reflected in distinct loading techniques.

The first step in loading the built-up gun was to ladle a measure of powder into the detachable breech piece and cover it with a wooden plug. Next, the ball was inserted into the breech end of the barrel, and the breech piece was slipped into grooves in the carriage. Then, to hold the breech piece secure, a stout wedge was pounded into place behind it with a mallet.

Because the cast gun had no detachable breech, it had to be loaded from the muzzle end. The powder charge—sometimes wrapped in a cloth cartridge—was ladled down

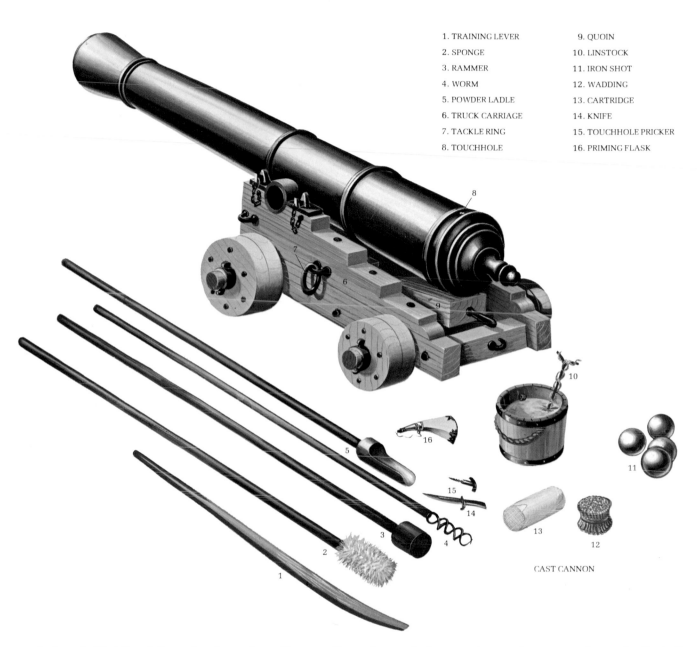

1. TRAINING LEVER
2. SPONGE
3. RAMMER
4. WORM
5. POWDER LADLE
6. TRUCK CARRIAGE
7. TACKLE RING
8. TOUCHHOLE
9. QUOIN
10. LINSTOCK
11. IRON SHOT
12. WADDING
13. CARTRIDGE
14. KNIFE
15. TOUCHHOLE PRICKER
16. PRIMING FLASK

CAST CANNON

the barrel. Wadding followed and was shoved home with a rammer. The wadding served the double purpose of securing the charge in the chamber and keeping it dry until use; the guns were often loaded in advance of battle. Next, the ball was rolled down the gun's throat.

Firing was the same for both guns. At the master gunner's command, the touchhole was pricked clean and primed with a daub of powder from a horn or a flask. The weapon was trained to the left or right with a lever applied to the rear of the carriage. A gun on a stock carriage could not be elevated, but one on a truck carriage could be raised or lowered about 20 degrees by means of a quoin. Last, the gunner applied a glowing linstock to the touchhole, and the cannon went off, its recoil checked by ropes running from the ship's side to tackle rings on the barrel or the carriage.

Of the two types of cannon, the cast-bronze piece cost more to produce and was therefore slower to come into general use. But it was inherently stronger; uncounted built-up cannon exploded on firing, causing terrible carnage among the gunners. By the close of the century, cast bronze was clearly ascendant—and it would be used for the major naval weapons of the next three centuries.

the wind to keep the flames from sweeping forward to a second powder store in the forecastle. Boats were sent in to take off the wounded and to recover the squadron's paymaster, along with some heavy coffers of the imperial gold that had been brought along to help finance the expected occupation of England. When the fires had been brought under control, the smoldering hulk was taken in tow by two galleasses.

By now dusk was falling and the wind was gusting in from the west, raising a mean chop in the Channel waters. The gusts brought the afternoon's second disaster. Pedro de Valdés, his bowsprit and spritsail dangling from his prow after the *Rosario's* recent collision, was having trouble steering. Some of the foremast rigging had also been damaged, and as the *Rosario* heaved and pitched in the rising sea, the mast began to crack and buckle. Suddenly it sheared off at the deck, falling aft into the mainmast and causing an impossible tangle of spars, hemp and canvas. The *Rosario* was immobilized. Don Pedro fired a distress signal; in response the Duke fired a cannon to stop the fleet for the second time that afternoon. Then he spun about to assist Don Pedro. A hawser was passed to the tossing ship, but as the line drew taut a sudden strain snapped it in two. With the wind and sea building up dangerously, there was no way to get a second line across.

A number of pinnaces were now clustering around the crippled ship, along with the squadron's almiranta and one of the galleasses. Aboard the *San Martín*, the Duke's chief of staff, Diego Flores de Valdés, assessed the situation with hardheaded logic. It was growing dark, he said, and in the foul weather the waiting fleet would drift out of formation. There might be other collisions, and some of the ships would certainly become scattered during the night. He urged the Duke to resume his station at the front of the Armada and continue upchannel toward his vague appointment with Parma. The almiranta, the galleass and a pinnace could be left to tend the *Rosario*.

Every instinct of Iberian pride and chivalry argued against abandoning a comrade in the field, but it seemed to be the only prudent course, and with great reluctance the Duke agreed. As the *San Martín* returned to the van, the Duke paced back and forth on the quarter-deck, munching a slice of cheese and some biscuit—the first food he had eaten since breakfast—and mulling over the two freak casualties that had beset him in quick succession. Later that evening, he heard the thud of cannon far astern, where the *Rosario* lay wallowing in the darkness; the English must have moved in for the kill. If Medina Sidonia felt a twinge of conscience for having abandoned his comrade, it would not have helped him at all to remember also that Diego Flores de Valdés, who had urged the flight upon him, was a bitter enemy of his cousin Pedro de Valdés, the abandoned captain.

The English fleet, its ranks swelling with late arrivals from Plymouth and with a stream of volunteer craft come out to view the action, moved into rough alignment to follow the Armada's advance upchannel. Drake's *Revenge* took the lead. Howard in the *Ark Royal* followed immediately behind, with a train of Queen's ships, armed merchantmen and small craft fanning out in ragged bunches farther back. As the twilight thickened, Drake's great stern lantern, the designated beacon for the fleet, winked on. The lights of Plymouth slipped astern, and the massed enemy sails ahead faded in the gray dusk until finally they vanished from view altogether.

Sometime after midnight, aboard the *Ark Royal*, Howard noted that Drake's flickering stern light, too, had disappeared. Making the best of it, Howard pressed ahead with two other Queen's ships, the 600-ton *Mary Rose* and the 1,000-ton *White Bear*. After a time, Howard detected the faint glimmer of a ship's light far to leeward; assuming that Drake had simply outdistanced him, he steered that way. As the sky lightened with Monday's dawn, he saw his mistake. He had been following the stern light of the weathermost Spanish galleon.

The main body of the English fleet was still miles away to the west, hull down on the windward horizon. Howard, having blundered almost to within cannon shot of the powerful Spanish rear guard, could only retreat. With his two companion vessels, he clawed back to the safety of his fleet.

One of the first ships to hail the *Ark Royal* was a small London privateer, the 200-ton *Margaret and John*. Her captain, John Fisher, bounded aboard the English flagship with an exciting tale to tell. The previous evening, as the fleet was following the Armada past Start Point, Fisher had sighted an enormous enemy ship, her bowsprit gone and her foremast teetering against her mainmast. Three other Spanish vessels were hovering nearby, but as he approached they turned and fled. Fisher stayed to investigate. Around 9 o'clock, having seen no sign of life, he drew close to the ship's towering sides and discharged a volley of musket fire. The ship thundered back with two cannon shot. The *Margaret and John* next let go a broadside, and then stood off to see what would happen. Fisher's little merchantman carried a crew of only 90 and very light armament, and he thought better of assaulting a 1,100-ton giant that had 46 guns and some 400 armed men aboard. Around midnight he left to catch up with the rest of the English fleet. Now Captain Fisher sought permission to return with reinforcements and claim his prize.

Before Lord Howard could answer, a pinnace sped up with another message—this one from Francis Drake himself, who had captured a Spanish command ship. During the night, the vice admiral explained, he had seen some mysterious sails approaching him to starboard, and so had peeled off to investigate. To avoid confusing the fleet, he had doused his stern light.

The mystery ships were only some German merchantmen, it turned out, but as the sun rose Drake had chanced to find himself hard by the dismasted *Rosario*. He sent out his boat, demanding immediate surrender. On what terms, the Spanish commander wanted to know? My own terms, Drake replied impatiently; he was "not now at leisure to make any long parle." Pedro de Valdés, on learning that it was Drake who confronted him, and "being moved with the renoune and celebritie of his name," an English chronicler recorded, yielded without firing a shot. Drake, always gallant toward captives, treated Don Pedro to "very honourable entertainment" aboard the *Revenge*; he fed him a hearty dinner

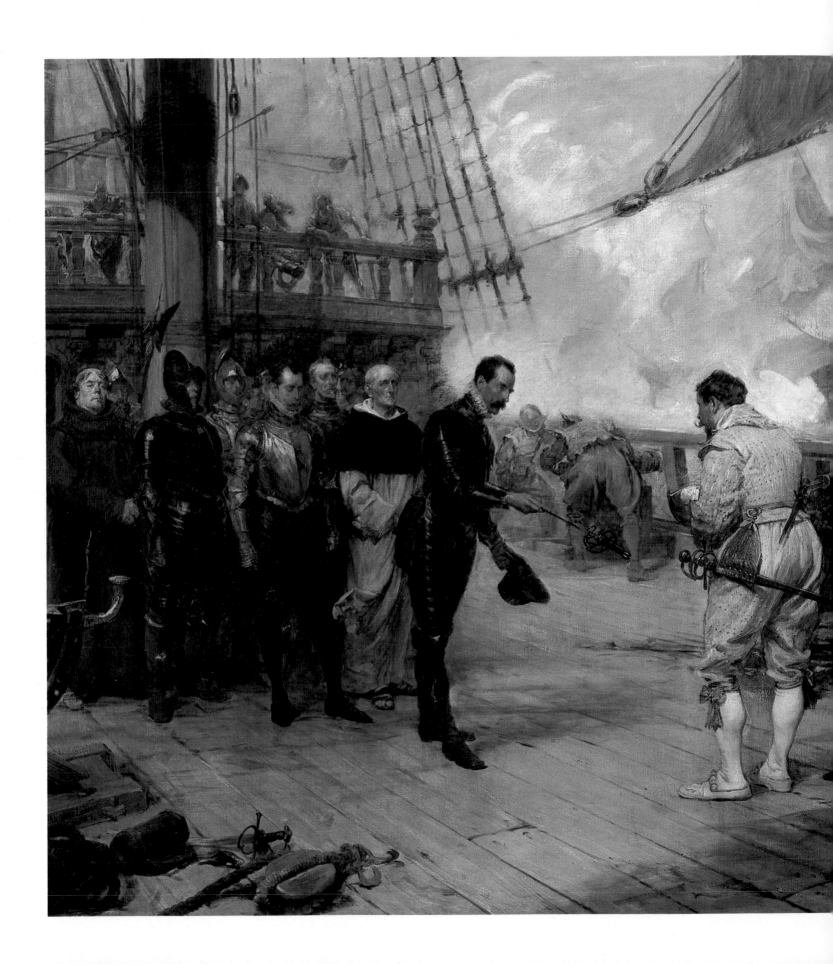

and offered the use of his own cabin. Meanwhile, the *Rosario* was towed into Tor Bay, to be relieved of her 46 cannon, her huge stores of powder and shot, and her treasure of 55,000 gold ducats.

The Lord Admiral must have felt a certain bemusement at Drake's report. His second-in-command had deserted his post, told no one what he was doing, left his admiral to blunder into the Spanish rear, and gone off to hunt prizes. Such a trick might be fair enough when freebooting, but in battle it was a rash breach of naval discipline. Still, this particular freebooter also happened to be one of the great leaders of the English fleet. Howard accepted Drake's story with generous equanimity, perhaps even with a secret smile. Just like the zestful, impetuous Drake to do such a thing.

In any event, Howard soon acquired a prize of his own. As the fleet continued once again in the wake of the Armada, Howard came upon the charred hulk of the *San Salvador*, which had been abandoned by the Spaniards and was beginning to sink. He sent John Hawkins and his cousin Thomas Howard to claim salvage. The job was not pleasant. The two men found the *San Salvador*'s decks caved in, piles of mangled bodies, and 50 Spanish seamen still dying of powder burns. "The stink in the ship was so unsavoury, and the sight within board so ugly," they reported, that they very quickly left. Thomas Fleming was detached in the *Golden Hind* to tow the remains into Weymouth. The spoils included, in addition to some pipes of wine and casks of rancid beef in the unburned forward hold, a treasure trove of munitions—132 barrels of powder and 2,246 rounds of shot. These goods, more valuable just now than rubies, were sent immediately to the admiral. He would soon need every last cannon ball and powder grain.

Word of the haul spread rapidly along the southern coast, and inland as well. Scores of volunteer citizens were eager to join in the action but lacked the ammunition to do so. Now they came thronging into the ports all along the Channel, commandeering every craft that would float, scarcely bothering to stock provisions or arms. There were merchants and squires, young bucks from court, militia captains from Cornwall and Devon and, according to one chronicler, a roster of great names that read like a Domesday Book of Elizabethan noblesse: the Earls of Oxford, Cumberland, Northumberland; Thomas Cecil, Lord Burghley's son; Sir Walter Raleigh, who had organized the Cornwall defenses; young Robert Carey, future Earl of Monmouth, who noted in his memoirs how he followed "the King of Spain's great Armada" as it "came upon our coast, thinking to devour us all." From all corners of the realm, the chronicler noted, eager citizens "came flocking thither as unto a set field, where

In a dramatic encounter re-created by a 19th Century artist, Pedro de Valdés, captain of the disabled Nuestra Señora del Rosario, surrenders to the white-garbed Francis Drake on board the Revenge. Valdés told Drake that he had "resolved to die in battle," but saw no dishonor in yielding to the greatest seaman of the age.

immortall fame and glory was to be attained, and faithfull service to bee performed unto their prince and countrey."

For every Englishman who put to sea, there were hundreds more who observed the progress of the fleets from the high bluffs and rolling green downs overlooking the English Channel. Throughout the day Monday, as the wind eased and the seas leveled, the onlookers watched the massed sails, gray in the distance, glide eastward at a stately two or three knots—rowboat speed.

The more astute among them might have noticed, during the day, a significant movement of ships in the Armada crescent. The Spaniards were shifting formation in order to stiffen their rear. Alonso de Leiva, posted until now in the van, moved back with the Levanters and four galleons from the Portuguese squadron. He would command the rear guard until Recalde had finished repairing Sunday's damage to the *San Juan de Portugal*. The rear now included 43 of Spain's best warships. Some 20 galleons and armed merchantmen remained in the van, led by Medina Sidonia in the *San Martín*. (Unknown to the onlookers, the Duke had devised a simple expedient to maintain the new formation: provost marshals went through the fleet with written orders to hang any captain who broke ranks.)

If the watchers on the downs wanted another spectacle of gun smoke, they would have to be patient; no battle took place that Monday. Throughout the afternoon the wind kept dropping, and toward sunset it failed entirely, leaving the two fleets adrift on a darkening sea, slightly more than a gunshot apart. To their left loomed the bulky profile of Portland Bill, a huge limestone crest connected by a thin sandspit to the mainland. Portland Bill is a notable Channel landmark and also the site of one of England's oldest stone quarries. Since medieval times, great limestone blocks have been cut from its seaward face to build castles, abbeys and fortresses, including the Tower of London.

Throughout the night Monday the ships drifted past the Bill with the tidal currents, first east, then west, and then back again. But at daybreak on Tuesday the water began to ripple, and the sails lifted on their yards. A breeze came from shore, blowing in fresh from the northeast. It brought joy to the Spaniards (for it gave the Armada the weather gauge) and consternation to the English. And to whatever observers were gathered on the bluffs of Portland Bill, it brought all the gun smoke they could have wished for.

Watching the start of the battle, they would have seen the English ships moving close-hauled to the north, toward land, in an attempt to outflank the Spanish left wing and recover the wind. As the Spaniards bore down to head them off, most of the English line came about and turned southeast toward the opposite wing.

Anyone standing at the outermost precipice of the Bill would have detected, directly under his feet, six English vessels that failed to turn. He might have recognized Martin Frobisher's *Triumph*, from her great size, and five smaller vessels. They were the *Merchant Royal*, the *Margaret and John*, the *Centurian* and the *Golden Lion*, all London merchantmen, and the Queen's ship *Mary Rose*. Frobisher, blocked to the south by the enemy and unable to weather the Bill, had apparently dropped an-

With her toppled foresail drooping over the bow, the captive Nuestra Señora del Rosario is towed by Drake's Revenge toward the English coast. The depiction reflects English enthusiasm for Drake's role in the capture—but such towing was actually left to minor vessels.

chor in order to avoid being carried onto the rocks by the seething currents. At the same time, the four Spanish galleasses drove up to assail the *Triumph* and her companions.

Whatever apprehension the observers may have felt as the galleasses approached would turn gradually to proud delight as the skirmish below progressed. The galleon *Triumph*, a toy ship at this distance, was England's largest warship, one of the few remaining vessels in the Queen's navy to carry high forecastles and sterncastles, and she had a murderous battery of 42 guns. Her broadsides fired into the banks of Spanish oars, splintering them like matchsticks. To keep steerageway the Spaniards raised sail, but the galleasses were not good sailers. With the current now working against them as it boiled past the Bill, and with Frobisher's gunners mowing down many of the rowers, they were unable to get close enough to do any real damage. The *Triumph*, with the merchantmen's help, was living up to her name.

The main engagement, hidden by distance and by the greatest outpouring of gun smoke yet to occur at sea, was difficult to follow even by the men who took part in it. It was managed, one scribe noted, "with confusion enough." The English tried repeatedly to maneuver to windward of the Spanish southern wing, without success. The opposing lines moved closer and closer, to cannon range, then to musket shot, and all the while the broadsides erupted so thick and fast that they seemed to the men on the ships like a continuous roll of giant musketry. "There was never seen a more terrible value of great shot," Lord Howard exclaimed, "nor more hot fight than this was."

The battle continued until about three in the afternoon, "very nobly," Howard thought, as he noted the clear superiority of the English gunners. They were outfiring the Spaniards at a rate of 3 to 1, by estimates from observers in both fleets. The English vessels "charged the Enemy with wonderfull Agility and Nimbleness," a chronicler related, "and having given their Broad-sides, presently stood off at a distance from them and levelled their Shot directly without missing at those great Ships of the Spaniards."

The English were helped by the wind, which in late morning began to shift, as land breezes often do. It veered to the east, then toward the south, until finally it favored the English with the weather gauge, blowing from seaward behind Howard's right flank. A detachment of ships under Drake boiled down toward the Spanish right wing. Howard, who

In another of Lord Admiral Howard's commissioned engravings of the invasion attempt, the bulk of the English fleet charges at the seaward side of the Spanish crescent off Portland Bill (1). Then, as the two fleets proceed upchannel, the English fall into four tight squadrons behind the Spaniards (2).

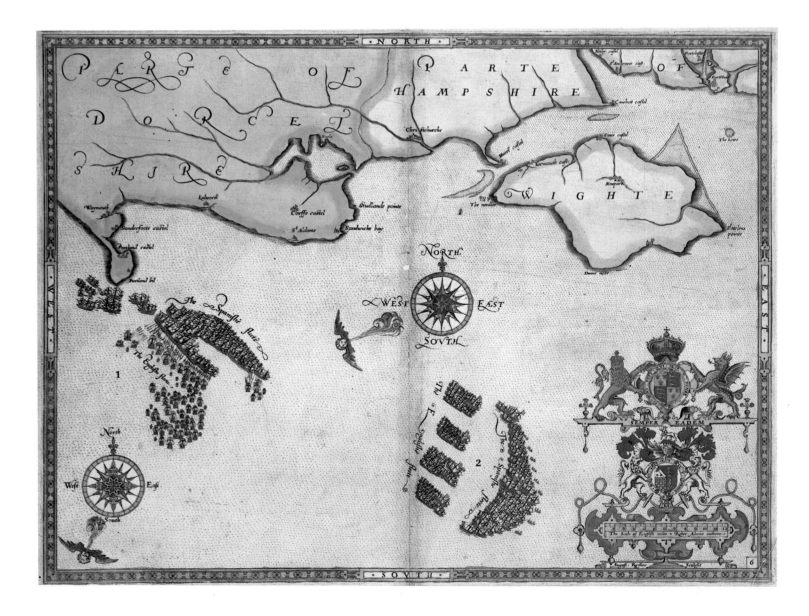

had been keeping a weather eye cocked toward Portland Bill, now turned north to relieve Frobisher.

Medina Sidonia had been trying all morning to bring Howard within grappling distance, and he refused to let up now. When he saw the English flagship heading north, the Duke led a line of 16 vessels to intercept her. Then he noticed an attack on his right: Recalde, who had patched up the damage to the *San Juan de Portugal*, was now being pounded by the guns of about a dozen English ships. The Duke detached his entire train of 16 ships to succor Recalde. His own ship held steadily north toward the *Ark Royal*. He would fight Howard alone, flagship to flagship, handstroke to handstroke.

Such solitary valor sprang from the highest traditions of Spanish gallantry, but on this occasion it was not wise. Howard sailed up to the *San Martín*, delivered a broadside—and then sailed on. So did the next ship behind him, and the next. The entire English line poured its fire at the astonished Duke, then doubled back and delivered a second series of broadsides. During the next hour the *San Martín* received some 500 shots, by the Duke's own count. Her sails were shredded, her hull was battered, her rigging smashed, her flagstaff carried away and the great banner that had been consecrated in Lisbon Cathedral rent in two. Medina Sidonia stood up to this punishment, daring Howard to grapple and board, until a line of Spanish galleons clawed up to his rescue. By this time Howard had used up most of his ammunition. The English admiral raised his signal flag, breaking off the action. The battle of Portland Bill had ended.

Like the battle of Plymouth, the Portland engagement brought slim comfort to either side. Howard found some satisfaction in the drubbing he had given the *San Martín*, but the fact remained that he had failed to put her out of action. The "terrible value of great shot" the English had fired, moreover, had left their lockers severely depleted. Howard sent a flock of pinnaces up and down the coast with urgent requests for fresh supplies of shot and powder. If no more cannon balls could be gathered, anything that could serve as missiles would do—plow chains or even chunks of scrap iron packed in leather pouches.

Medina Sidonia did not even have Howard's slim satisfaction. "A fine day this has been!" he told Hugo de Moncada, commander of the galleasses, as the Armada continued its majestic crawl upchannel with the English tagging at its heels. "These people do not mean to fight, but only to delay our progress." At his every attempt to grapple and board, the English had evaded him—"by reason of the lightness of their vessels," he said. Even so, he had lost some 50 men to enemy fire. In the meantime, Medina Sidonia had another nagging worry; he had not yet heard from Parma, although he had continued to send messengers to Dunkirk every day. When and where would the rendezvous take place? Was Parma even ready for it?

Wednesday morning brought a minor skirmish, brief but hot, as a light westerly gentled the fleets toward the Isle of Wight. During the night the tublike *Gran Grifón*, flagship of the supply urcas, had drifted to the rear of the Spanish right wing. Drake—whose knack for being at the right place at the right time seemed positively uncanny—was close by and swooped down upon her. The *Gran Grifón* piled on canvas but she was an awkward sailer. Drake easily caught up. He blasted her with first one broadside, then another, then crossed her stern to rake her decks. Other English ships glided up and encircled the unfortunate urca. She fought back bravely, her 38 guns blazing.

Eventually she got some assistance from Recalde, Oquendo, Leiva and Bertendona, all of whom had turned back at the sound of gunfire. A galleass stroked up to heave the *Gran Grifón* a line—she was far too battered to sail on her own—and drew her into the safety of the crescent. The gun duel continued for perhaps another hour, until Medina Sidonia arrived with the vanguard galleons. At this show of force, Drake withdrew. His main yard was shot away, and he had suffered some casualties. The Spanish suffered heavier losses: 60 dead and 70 wounded, their worst day so far.

On Wednesday afternoon the breeze again dropped to nothing, leaving the two fleets adrift near the western tip of the Isle of Wight. Howard feared the Spanish would attempt a landing here—and here Medina Sidonia had resolved to stand fast until he received a response from Parma. Without wind to move the ships, a landing was of course impossible. The two commanders could only slide east with the current, their sails hanging lifeless as bed sheets.

Howard took advantage of the enforced idleness to call his captains to a war council. Whatever their opinion of the enemy's gunnery, the English were thoroughly impressed by the discipline with which the Spanish ships kept formation. Howard's own galleons had been darting about in disorganized gaggles, following the Lord Admiral, or Drake, or any leader more or less at whim. Perhaps a more disciplined grouping would add punch to the English attack. Taking a cue from the Spaniards, Howard divided his fleet into four squadrons of approximately 25 ships each. He would command one squadron himself; Drake would take another; the third would go to John Hawkins; and Martin Frobisher, whose superb gunnery aboard the *Triumph* had put on such a show at Portland Bill, would lead the fourth squadron. That night they would test their new deployment in a daring maneuver. At a common signal, six armed merchantmen from each squadron would spurt forward in the darkness and—"to keep the enemy waking"—would assault the Spanish rear. If the wind came up, that is.

It never did. By next morning the fleets had wafted perhaps a dozen miles east, still only a mile apart. Keeping formation without benefit of steerageway was an almost impossible task for either side, and once again there were a few stragglers among the Spanish ships. The frontline Portuguese galleon *San Luis* and a West India merchantman, the *Duquesa Santa Ana*, were drifting close together, midway between the two fleets. The nearest English squadron was Hawkins'. Deprived of his adventure the night before, Hawkins did not let a mere calm stop him now. He ordered out his boats and had his ships towed toward the lagging Spaniards. Soon musket fire from the enemy mast tops began splattering the water around the oarsmen.

The Spaniards had the perfect weapon for this type of dead-calm encounter: the galleass. Three galleasses now came boiling up, bringing Leiva's heavily gunned *Rata* in tow for extra firepower. Lord Howard, in the meantime, inspired by Hawkins' ingenious drive, ordered out his own longboats. Followed by his kinsman Thomas Howard in the *Golden Lion*, he broke from his own formation and had his vessel towed down to the action.

The great galleons thundered away at each other at a standstill. Only the galleasses were able to move about. These vessels, being less solidly built than the sailing ships, took some slight punishment. Howard boasted later that one of the galleasses had been holed, that "another by a shot from the *Ark* lost her lantern, which came swimming by, and the third his nose. After which time the galleasses were never seen in fight any more, so bad was their entertainment in this encounter." Euphoria got the better of Howard; in fact, the crews of the galleasses managed to string lines to the *Duquesa Santa Ana* and the *San Luis*, and to haul the two ships neatly back into the main fleet.

While the galleasses were towing the Armada stragglers to safety, a

As the Armada hovers dangerously close to the Isle of Wight in a dead calm, the fleets prepare to join in battle; towed by small boats, the English galleons move toward the enemy, while the Spanish galleasses pull away from the crescent under the power of oarsmen.

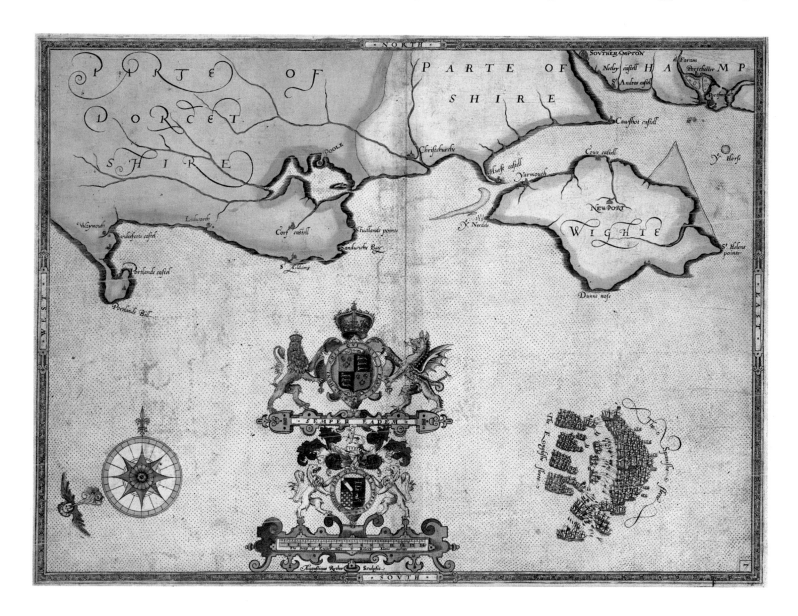

second engagement broke out at the fleet's northern wing. As at Portland Bill, the English commander on this side was Martin Frobisher. During the night Frobisher had edged his squadron toward the Isle of Wight and, pushed along by the powerful inshore current, had slipped ahead of the Spanish left wing. By morning he was slightly northeast of the wing, in a position to resist any Spanish attempt to land or to seize an anchorage in the Solent.

Light puffs of morning air were drifting out from land, enough to carry Frobisher and his ships back down toward the weathermost Spaniards. Flashes of gunfire erupted from both squadrons, and smoke hung lazily in sails and rigging. As the two sides traded volleys, Spanish reinforcements began moving up, led by the *San Martín*. Frobisher eased down to challenge the Duke. For the next half hour the *Triumph* and the *San Martín* blasted each other, broadside to broadside. Frobisher, enjoying a slight windward advantage, seemed to be in businesslike control. But then the wind began veering into the south, as had happened at Portland Bill.

Frobisher was now in trouble. The remainder of his squadron, catching the wind shift first, turned westward in order to reach back around the Spanish wing. The *Triumph* was the last English ship to the east; she would almost certainly be cut off by the advancing Spanish warships. The only alternatives Frobisher had, it seemed, were to make a suicidal stand against the full enemy squadron, or else to beat an ignominious retreat into the Solent.

But Frobisher did neither. He was a stubborn and adroit campaigner, and he was not the type to give in to anyone. His response to this crisis was to call out his longboats. At whatever cost in energy and blood, he would haul himself past the enemy to safety and the weather gauge. His squadron mates sent longboats to help, and soon the *Triumph* was inching forward behind a string of 11 straining boats' crews. Suddenly the wind gusted stronger. Frobisher cut loose from his tow, shook out his sails, and made a dash past the Spanish wing to rejoin his squadron. The Spaniards took off after him in pursuit. To the Armada's chief purser, Pedro Coco Calderón, it seemed that they need not have bothered. He looked on wonderingly as the English galleon "got out so swiftly that the galleon *San Juan de Portugal* and another quick-sailing ship—the speediest vessels in the Armada—seemed in comparison with her to be standing still."

The fighting now extended in sporadic bursts along the entire front between the two fleets. Billows of gun smoke enfolded the Armada's seaward tip as Drake, with the southernmost English squadron, charged down before the freshening southwest wind. The 34-gun *San Mateo*, one of the large Portuguese galleons, bore the initial rush. An even larger galleon, the 900-ton *Florencia*, then moved into the front position. She was brand-new, built the year before by the Grand Duke of Tuscany for the East India spice trade and impounded at Lisbon for service in the Armada. She mounted a battery of 52 guns, more armament than any other Armada ship, and held her own very nicely. As the gun duel continued, however, and as the wind and current caught and pushed the battling ships, the Spanish right wing began to sag slightly to the north-

DVNNE.NOSE.

Raising their sails to catch a reviving breeze, English galleons dispense with the longboats that had been towing them and head for a fight with a cluster of oared Spanish galleasses (lower left).

east. The ships behind it and those toward the center were jostled, so that the entire Armada was gently nudged across the mouth of the Solent and toward the English mainland.

There is no record that the English captains had consciously plotted this maneuver. Perhaps it was simply the happenstance of war and weather. But if planned, it was brilliant. As the Spanish ships drifted east, the entrance to the Solent bore increasingly to windward of them. Had they wanted to seize the anchorage, they could no longer have done so. Furthermore, the shoreline to the east shelved off in a nasty confusion of underwater snags and rocks, the Owers, which extended several miles into the Channel. Before the Spaniards knew what was happening, the Armada was being herded straight onto the Owers.

Medina Sidonia's charts may not have shown what was there, but one look at the green, roiled water to leeward must have signaled disaster. The Duke called a sudden cease-fire, gathered his fleet and sped south toward open water. He had acted just in time; another half hour, and the Armada would have fetched up on the rocks.

The battle of the Isle of Wight had ended in another draw. The English nonetheless pronounced the engagement a victory and celebrated it as such. Friday dawned calm and sunny, a superb August day, and Howard invited a few chosen senior officers to the *Ark* for an impromptu ceremony. One by one, as the officers knelt before him on the quarter-deck, the Lord Admiral touched them on the shoulder with his sword and, exercising the authority of his commission, bestowed knighthoods all around. The decorations went to John Hawkins, master architect of English sea power; Martin Frobisher, for his heroism at Portland Bill and the Isle of Wight; Lord Thomas Howard of the *Golden Lion* and Lord Edmund Sheffield of the *White Bear*, both of whom had shown exceptional valor in the Channel fights; and Roger Tounshend, for special services (their nature is not known). Only Drake received no knighthood—but then he already had one, granted seven years earlier by the Queen herself. Howard could hardly top that.

The rest of the day was spent restocking victuals and ammunition. Shot and powder had been arriving in driblets from forts and castles along the coast, barely enough to carry the fleet through each day's battle. Much more would be needed as the Armada approached the Dover Strait. Here at the Channel's narrow eastern exit, with a scant 20 miles of water separating England from continental Europe, was the most likely point for the Armada and Parma's invasion force to rendezvous. Here a final stand would have to be made.

To alert the rest of the fleet, Howard had already sent a dispatch boat east to Lord Henry Seymour, the admiral who was stationed at Dover, where he guarded the far end of the Channel with 35 sail. Seymour was known to be impatient for a real fight. His current assignment—helping the Dutch Sea Beggars blockade the Flanders coast—gave him little opportunity for gallantry, and he had complained noisily that he was "most sorry that I am so tied I cannot be an actor in the play." Now Howard summoned Seymour and his next-in-command, William Wynter, to join him in a final onslaught against the Armada.

Medina Sidonia moved on up the Channel with an increasingly heavy heart. The past week had brought little glory or satisfaction. As the Armada slipped east past the English coast, the enemy close on its tail, he felt a gnawing sensation that it was he, not Howard, who was retreating. He had lost no major battles, to be sure. His casualties had been light—only 167 killed and 241 wounded in all four skirmishes. He had lost not a single ship, except for those two freak mishaps with the *Rosario* and the *San Salvador* on the very first day. But he had won no victories, either. What could he do against a craven opponent who refused to stand and fight, who kept darting up to pelt his wings with great shot, then turned and fled when challenged?

The Channel skirmishes had put a heavy tax not only on Medina Sidonia, but on the energies and morale of his entire fleet as well. Six days of constant watchfulness, of heavy cannonading, of intricate maneuvering in strange waters, of meals skipped and sleep caught in snatches, were wearing down both officers and men. Like Howard, the Duke also faced a worrisome shortage of heavy ammunition. The Armada still had plenty of lead for musket and harquebus shot, and plenty of

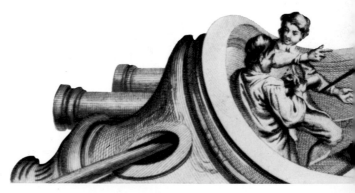

In this detail from an 18th Century
engraving commemorating the
English triumph over the Armada, the
winged figure of Victory surmounts
a pillar adorned with the beaks of ships
while Lord Howard bestows knighthood
on five of his favorite captains.

high-grade powder, but the supply of great shot was severely depleted. On Friday morning, as Howard was knighting his captains, Medina Sidonia was dispatching yet another pinnace to Dunkirk, this time asking Parma for a quick transfusion of culverin shot. He also begged Parma to send him some ships—40 or 50 fast, shallow-draft flyboats of the type he assumed to be plentiful in Flanders. The flyboats, he felt, would be better suited than his own heavy warships for catching the agile, elusive English. He ended with a reprise of the worry that had been nagging him: We must name a rendezvous—make ready to join the Armada the minute it appears off Dunkirk.

Friday evening, August 5, brought a change in the weather. The sky clouded over and the wind picked up hard and cold from the west. All night the Armada scudded before it, the English fleet trailing a mile or two behind. Saturday morning saw the two fleets nearing the Dover Strait. At 10 a.m., in a gusty drizzle, the Armada lookouts sighted the coast of France, near Boulogne. By four in the afternoon the Armada had come abreast of Calais. If the fleet kept going, the Duke's pilots cautioned, the powerful local currents would carry it through the strait, out into the North Sea and away from England. Heeding their counsel, the Duke gave the order to anchor at 5 p.m.

The ships dropped into a broad, open roadstead outside the Calais breakwater. Leaning over the *San Martín*'s taffrail, the Duke could watch the English squadrons, now reinforced by 35 ships under Seymour and Wynter. As his own anchor caught, swinging his bow into the wind, he could see the lead English galleons rounding up and striking their sails, just a long culverin shot away. With the enemy close on his rear, with his ally up ahead still inexplicably silent, the Duke could not imagine what might happen next.

Chapter 5

Denouement at Gravelines

rom the Calais breakwater to the entrance of Dunkirk harbor is a distance of only 20 nautical miles. The French town and the Flemish one are near neighbors, separated by not much more than the fishing village of Gravelines in Flanders, and by the shifting underwater contours of the Flemish sandbanks. But to the Duke of Medina Sidonia and the Duke of Parma, the two Spanish commanders in charge of the Enterprise of England, the ports might as well have been a universe apart. So bad had communications been between the two men that the Armada was already fighting its second battle, the one off Portland Bill on the 2nd of August, before the Duke of Parma even knew that the fleet had arrived in English waters.

The word finally came to him from Rodrigo Tello de Guzmán, the first of a series of messengers Medina Sidonia had dispatched to Flanders. Tello had left the admiral more than a week before, at the entrance to the English Channel. He had sailed by pinnace through the storm that had scattered the Spanish fleet just short of Cornwall, and had pushed on to Dunkirk, one of the two designated points of embarkation for Parma's land forces. What he discovered there shocked him. No army of invasion troops was in sight. Neither was there any crack squadron of flyboats such as the admiral was expecting. A mere handful of open-deck canal barges lay tied up at the Dunkirk quay—pitifully small and weak they seemed, with no guns mounted and no masts stepped. The Duke of Parma himself was nowhere to be found; to reach the general, Tello was told, he would have to travel another 40 miles up the coast to Parma's headquarters in Bruges.

When Tello arrived there, the general greeted him with all due courtesy. He was delighted, he said, that the Armada had finally arrived. There was no cause for alarm; he had some gunboats stationed farther up the coast, at Antwerp; and plenty of troop barges that lay hidden along the canals could be quickly readied for launching. The Duke declared that his infantry battalions—5,600 troops already at Nieuport and 15,300 more garrisoned at Dixmude, a short march inland—could be embarked in about six days. Tello was not convinced. On the 6th of August, as he trekked back through Dunkirk on his way to rejoin Medina Sidonia and the fleet, he saw no visible sign of increased preparedness. Two weeks at the soonest, he thought.

In fact, Parma was dissembling. First of all, the news of the Armada's arrival had caught him completely by surprise. He had known that the fleet was coming, but he had no idea when. Just three weeks earlier, bets on the Paris Bourse had been running 6 to 1 against the Spaniards' reaching England anytime that summer. The message that

In a swirl of flames, gun smoke and roiled waters, Spanish and English seamen engage in the climactic encounter between their countries' fleets off the Flemish village of Gravelines on August 8, 1588. This romanticized rendering was painted two centuries after the fact.

Tello had brought for him from Medina Sidonia was the first direct communication that he had received from the admiral in more than a month, and the first definite report that the Armada had even left Corunna. No wonder Parma was not quite ready for it.

There was still another reason for Parma's lack of preparedness. During the long months of waiting, as the general pondered the whys and wherefores of the Enterprise of England, his early enthusiasm had begun to wilt. In his reports to King Philip he began citing all the reasons why the invasion plan might not work. There was not enough money to build the required number of barges and gunboats, nor to feed and equip his troops. His men were becoming increasingly restless and intractable as the months passed. The Flemish conscripts, who were supposed to fit out and operate the boats, were being particularly troublesome. When pay ran short they would lay down their tools and refuse to continue working; many of them, reported one chronicler, had simply "withdrawn themselves and slunk away."

That was not all. The barges were flimsy craft, and when launching them Parma would require close and powerful naval support. Would he get it? "Four ships of war could sink every one of my boats," he advised Philip. At one point he went so far as to urge Philip to make terms with Elizabeth, to call off the Enterprise, and end the "misery and calamity" in the Netherlands. "This would be better than risking the Armada in an adventure," he declared.

Parma's behavior remains one of the lasting enigmas of the Armada story. No question about it, the general did face some nasty problems. Perhaps, as Europe's most astute and energetic soldier, he might have been able to triumph over them. No one knows. But dark hints began to circulate that the general had experienced a personal falling-out with Philip, that he had been promised the throne of England and that the promise had then been retracted. A corresponding rumor had it that the general was working on a secret deal with Elizabeth, a deal that would make him King of an independent Netherlands. But again, who knows? No proof remains.

A perfectly valid reason for the general's reluctance should have been evident to anyone who took the trouble to look for it, however. The invasion plan showed a serious tactical flaw: The all-important rendezvous of troop barges and Armada ships was unworkable.

Parma could hardly escape such a conclusion whenever he stood on the Dunkirk quay and gazed seaward; across the hazardous maze of shoals and sand flats that stretched away from the coast, a dozen miles broad in places, he could see a parade of hostile sails. Sometimes the sails belonged to Henry Seymour's Dover squadron. More often they marked the flyboats of the Dutch Sea Beggars. If the Armada's lumbering, deep-draft galleons were to try chasing the flyboats in among the shoals, they would run aground a dozen miles from shore. But without inshore support, how would Parma break through the stubborn Dutch blockade and conduct his barges to the mid-Channel rendezvous that the plan called for?

Time and again the general had explained the problem in his reports to Philip. The Armada would have to bring along its own squadron of

The title page of The Mariners Mirrour, an atlas containing 45 charts of European coastlines, features two sailors lowering sounding leads amid a potpourri of nautical instruments. First issued in 1584 in Dutch, the atlas was translated into English at the behest of England's highest naval authority, Lord Howard.

THE MARINERS MIRROVR

Wherin may playnly be seen the courses, heights, distances, depths, soundings, flouds and ebs, risings of lands, rocks, sands and shoalds, with the marks for th'entrings of the Harbouroughs, Havens and Ports of the greatest part of Europe: their seueral traficks and commodities. Together with the Rules and instrumēts of NAVIGATION.

First made & set fourth in diuers exact Sea-Charts, by that famous Nauigator LVKE WAGENAR of Enchuisen. And now fitted with necessarie additions for the use of Englishmen by ANTHONY ASHLEY.

Heerin also may be understood the exploits lately atchiued by the right Honorable the L. Admiral of England with her Ma.tie Nauie and some former seruices don by that worthy Knight S.r FRA.s DRAKE.

Theodore de bry fecit

flyboats in order to cover the launch. But Philip was apparently not paying attention. And over the months, reading sporadic missives from Medina Sidonia, Parma began to suspect that the admiral had not absorbed the message either.

With grave reservations, then, the Duke of Parma dutifully cranked up the process that would aim his army across the Dover Strait toward England. As soon as he received the message brought by Tello, he went through all the proper motions. The 21,000 troops at Nieuport and Dixmude were placed on alert. The barges were brought up through the canals to the embarkation docks at Dunkirk and Nieuport. Gunboats were sent from Antwerp into the Scheldt River in an attempt to divert the blockading Dutch. A deputy governor general was summoned to Bruges to take over the Flanders government.

All the while more messengers kept arriving from Medina Sidonia, each one revealing more clearly that the admiral was unaware of the difficulties that lay ahead. His second emissary, Ensign Juan Gil, reached Bruges on Friday, the 5th of August, bearing a note that described the gun battle that had taken place five days earlier off the coast of Plymouth, inquired about the rendezvous site and asked Parma for some pilots to guide the Armada along the Flemish coast. "Without them," read the admiral's letter, "I do not know where I can find shelter for ships as large as these, in case I should be overtaken by the slightest storm." Preposterous, of course. Except for Antwerp, nowhere in Flanders was there a port that was wide enough or deep enough to accommodate the Armada.

Equally unrealistic messages followed in quick succession. A pinnace from Medina Sidonia arrived the following evening, reporting the fleet's advance to the Isle of Wight, and urgently requesting powder and shot. "By God's grace, if the wind serve, I expect to be on the Flemish coast very soon," the admiral wrote. On Sunday, the 7th of August, there came a plaintive demand for "40 or 50 flyboats"—as if Parma had flyboats to spare—"to resist the enemy's fleet until your Excellency can come out with the rest." And on Sunday evening another messenger arrived on horseback to announce the arrival of the Armada at Calais.

"God be praised for this!" the general wrote to King Philip, in a display of pious zeal he scarcely could have felt. But he reiterated his doubts about the task before him, explaining just why, at such short notice, he was still not quite ready to move. His boats were so small, he said, "that it is impossible to keep the troops on board them for long. There is no room to turn around, and the men would certainly fall ill, rot and die." The weather—wet and stormy now, with rain squalls galloping in from the west and the seas crashing against the sand flats in a fury of white water—could not have been worse. "This wind would prevent our boats from coming out, even if the sea were clear of the enemy's ships," he wrote.

Nevertheless, Parma began the embarkation he believed to be senseless. On Monday evening he marched to Nieuport and managed to herd 16,000 reluctant troopers into the barges. At Dunkirk the next morning he watched, sleepless and grim-faced, as more troops crowded aboard the barges there. One boat was so unseaworthy that it sank to the bottom

Seigneur de Gourdan, the Governor of Calais, took no sides in the Armada campaign, but found it profitable to allow the Spaniards to reprovision— at exorbitant prices—when they anchored off his shores. He lost his leg in a battle in which he and 50 fellow French adventurers wrested the Channel port from English possession in 1558.

of the canal, plunging the bewildered occupants into water up to their necks. In the midst of the confusion another messenger arrived from Medina Sidonia and began ranting because the launching was not completed. And all the while, reports flooded in of a rumbling of artillery at sea to the west, off Gravelines. The bloodiest battle of the Enterprise of England was under way.

The first messenger, Rodrigo Tello, returned to Medina Sidonia, now at Calais, as the sun rose on Sunday, August 7. He had sailed during the night in a dispatch boat from Dunkirk, and his account of the preparations there plunged the already worried admiral into deep gloom. No boats were ready, no soldiers had been embarked, Parma was still at Bruges—there would be no launch for two weeks at the earliest. With provisions and ammunition running dangerously low and the English lurking right on the horizon, two weeks was far longer than the Armada could afford to wait.

Moreover, Calais was no place to linger. The roadstead was unprotected; it was open to every prevailing wind and it was crossed by tidal currents and countercurrents. The admiral viewed his position as virtually indefensible.

One bright moment had occurred the previous evening—but even that was a mixed blessing. As soon as the Armada had dropped anchor, Medina Sidonia had sent his greetings to the Governor of Calais, Girault de Mauléon, Seigneur de Gourdan. The Governor was already waiting for him, having driven down to the beach in a carriage with his wife, who was eager to see a battle. Gourdan seemed friendly enough and was able to give some assistance; he could not spare any powder or ammunition, but he did offer to supply the Spaniards with fresh vegetables and medicines.

All through the day Sunday, while produce lighters plied back and forth between the port and the roadstead, the Spanish lookouts searched the English ships—still in sight a few miles away—for any sign of activity. At about 4 o'clock in the afternoon an enemy pinnace sailed down between the lines, sent four cannon blasts directly into the *San Martín* (doing no harm), and bustled back to windward with no more damage to herself than a tear in her topsail. She was a reconnaissance boat in all likelihood, come to study the disposition of the Spanish ships and the set of the current near the shore—an indication, perhaps, that trouble was brewing. The incident "was much noted for its daring impertinence," said a Spanish observer. Around sunset the lookouts thought they saw nine new ships join the fleet. They also counted a squadron of 26 sail shifting closer to land, for reasons that they could only guess at.

The gravest danger to the anchored Armada was from attack by fire ships. These dreaded vessels, loaded with gunpowder, pitch and other combustibles, were the classic weapon against a fleet in harbor. Almost everything about a 16th Century wooden warship—its canvas sails, its tarred rigging, its sun-dried decks and spars—was highly flammable. When such a vessel became entangled with a fire ship, it was almost certain to be consumed.

While a cluster of Spanish and English galleons battle at close range (left foreground), a squadron of flaming English fire ships—driven along by both a stiff wind and a strong tide—surges into the heart of the Armada anchorage of Calais.

The death-dealing powers of fire ships had increased exponentially in the last few years. Every man in the fleet knew what had happened in 1585, when the Dutch Sea Beggars had tried to lift the Spanish siege of Antwerp by sending the latest version of these feared instruments into the Scheldt River (page 36). "Devil ships," the Spaniards called these incendiary horrors, or "mine machines"; their hulls were reinforced with brick chambers into which more than three tons of explosives were packed. One such devil ship had fetched up against a fortified bridge across the Scheldt at Antwerp and blown it sky-high, killing 800 men, wounding untold hundreds more and spewing destruction over a half-mile radius. The designer of these hell-burners had been an Italian engineer named Federigo Giambelli. Giambelli was in London now, working for the English.

The best defense against a fire attack was to snag the approaching ships with hooks and towlines, and draw them away before they could reach the fleet. Failing that, the target would somehow have to maneuver itself out of the path of the oncoming fire ships. On Sunday evening, Medina Sidonia ordered a screen of pinnaces and longboats, equipped with grapnels and towlines, to stand guard upwind from the fleet. He also alerted his captains to be prepared to slip their cables— each ship had set two anchors because of the current—should the fire ships penetrate the screen. The cables were to be buoyed, he said, so that the captains would be able to return and pick up their anchors after the fire ships had burned themselves out.

That evening the wind piped up strong from the southwest, sending clouds scudding across the moon. Around midnight the tide began to come in. As it did, a flicker of orange light appeared at the edge of the English fleet. It was joined by a second light, then another, then still more lights, all moving downwind fast toward the jumbled masts of the Armada. Soon the Spaniards could count eight blazing hulks driving toward them in a tight rank, each vessel no more than two pikes' length away from its neighbor. The pinnaces beat their way forward to intercept them. The Spanish boats managed to hook the two outermost fire ships and tow them aside. But there was not enough time to deflect the six remaining vessels. The burning phalanx came on so suddenly, the wind and tide strong behind it, that within minutes it had reached the Armada's perimeter. Great thundering blasts shot out from the gunports, and the terrifying sound told the Spaniards that these could be no ordinary fire ships. Surely they must be the infernal mine machines of engineer Giambelli.

Panic swept the Spanish fleet. The captains cut their cables, hoisted their sails and ran. No one bothered with buoys; the anchors were simply abandoned where they were.

In a desperate effort to keep the fleet under control, Medina Sidonia steered the San Martín on a short tack northward, then turned back toward the Calais roadstead to drop his sheet anchor about a mile from his original berth. He clearly expected the fleet to follow. Four other first-rank vessels did. They were Miguel de Oquendo's Santa Ana, the galleon San Juan from the Castilian squadron, and the Portuguese galleons San Marcos and San Mateo. The rest of the Spanish ships dis-

Dealing death by fire

Elizabethan makers of war applied their ingenuity to any number of contrivances that were designed to destroy the foe by fire. One was an adaptation of the flaming arrow—a favorite device of antiquity—for use with the contemporary harquebus, giving the missile added range and velocity. Another was the grenade, a metal container filled with gunpowder; when hurled from a mortar, it would explode on contact. And if sabotage was the intent, a delayed incendiary blow could be dealt to enemy ships by a fire pot, a clay container perforated to hold slow-burning matches that would ignite gunpowder inside.

Although promising enough in theory, most of these weapons were less than reliable, and sensible commanders took a dim view of them. As one English officer put it, "Those inventions are naught because so dangerous, and not easie to bee quenched; and their practise worse, because they may doe as much mischiefe to a friend as to an enemy, therefore I will leave them as they are."

A soldier prepares to launch a fiery arrow from his harquebus. Flames traveling down the spiraled match cord accelerated in flight.

Sabotaging the enemy, a seaman nails a fire pot to the hull of a ship while his comrade gets ready to hand him another.

persed helter-skelter and, pushed along by the rising wind, scattered among the shoal-strewn shores of the English Channel. Many of them carried no spare anchor to set had they wanted to.

During the next few dark, fitful hours before dawn, the Duke could watch the glowing skeletons of the eight English fire ships as they burned out harmlessly on the Calais beach. They were not mine machines after all, just ordinary sailing craft that had been soaked in tar and resin, sprinkled with gunpowder and set alight. The terrifying broadside explosions had merely been double charges of shot and powder, loaded for effect; they had blasted off when the ships' cannon had overheated in the consuming flames.

The dawn on Monday, August 8, gray and blustery, sent a spasm of joy through the English fleet. In a week of cannonading in the Channel the Englishmen had failed to make even a dent in the solid bastion of the Armada battle formation. Now the Armada was thoroughly dispersed. Only six Spanish vessels remained in sight. There was the San Martín and her company of four galleons. In addition, the flagship galleass, the San Lorenzo, could be seen limping slowly inshore toward Calais harbor. In the headlong confusion of the night, the San Lorenzo had run foul of a neighbor's anchor cable and had smashed her rudder. Thus crippled, she made a most tempting prize.

Lord Howard fired a cannon, signaling anchors aweigh. With banners rippling and trumpets braying, the full English fleet—some 140 sail now—sped off in pursuit of the vanished enemy. Drake's squadron took the lead, followed by Frobisher, Hawkins, then the Dover squadron under Seymour and Wynter. Howard hung back. He would pause to finish off the San Lorenzo.

Howard led his squadron toward the wounded galleass, and soon great shot from the Ark Royal's bow chasers was pocking the water between the two vessels. The galleass, playing on the advantage of her relatively shallow draft, slipped out of range and into a shoal area close to shore, her 300 galley slaves flailing the choppy water with their giant sweeps. Suddenly she stopped dead. She had run hard aground on a sandbar just outside the harbor jetty. The tide was ebbing fast, a heavy surf pounded the shoal, and as the ocean drained away the San Lorenzo began to list onto her starboard side, her deck tilting toward shore and her port broadside pointing uselessly skyward. She lay as effectively stranded as a beached whale.

The English had driven the galleass out of action, but they had not yet collected their prize. Unable to reach the sandbar in the deepdraft Ark Royal, Howard lowered his longboat with a boarding party of some 60 soldiers. He would take the San Lorenzo by hand-to-hand assault. Various other ships in his squadron followed suit. One, the little Margaret and John, edged in too close, ran aground herself, then sent out a pinnace full of musketeers under her lieutenant, Richard Tomson. The Ark's longboat and Tomson's pinnace reached the galleass ahead of the others and began peppering the upturned hull with musket fire. The odds seemed heavily one-sided, as Tomson told it, "they being ensconced within their ship and very high over us, we in our open pinnaces and far under them, having nothing to shroud and cover us; they being 300 soldiers, and we not, at the instant, 100 persons." But Tomson and his men entered upon what he called "a pretty skirmish with our small shot against theirs."

Soon other English boats pulled up to join the fray. The attackers attempted to scramble up the galleass's towering seaward side, but they were driven back by a fusillade of small-arms fire from above. Crumpled bodies of dead and wounded Englishmen began to fill the boats. After half an hour or more of profitless bloodshed, it looked as though the English might be forced to withdraw. Then all of a sudden the balance changed. A lucky shot caught the Spanish commander, Hugo de Moncada, right between the eyes, and as he expired on his quarter-deck all resistance evaporated.

Most of the defenders took to their heels and tumbled over the low landward rail and into the surf. "Some escaped with being wet," Tomson noted wryly, "some, and that very many, were drowned." A few courageous Spaniards stayed behind to continue the fight, but by now their position was hopeless. At length, two of the leaders tied white handkerchiefs around their rapiers in a formal gesture of surrender. The English swarmed aboard. They quickly began pilfering every movable, salable object in sight.

All during the skirmish the good burghers of Calais had stood by watching—"in multitudes upon the shore," Tomson said—waiting to see what would happen. Now they moved into action. "So soon as they saw us possessed of so princely a vessel, the very glory and stay of the Spanish army," the lieutenant continued, the burghers evidently felt entitled to a share of the loot. It was their sandbar upon which the galleass had grounded, after all. A deputation arrived from the Calais Governor to make the city's claim.

"What is your pleasure?" demanded Tomson.

"We beheld your fight and rejoice in your victory," the head of the French delegation answered. "For your prowess and manhood, you well deserve the spoil and pillage of the galleass."

But he ordered Tomson not to take the ship or her guns; they belonged to the French. For emphasis, he needed only to point to the culverins of the Calais fort, looming just a few hundred yards distant across the beach and aimed directly at the *San Lorenzo*.

Against this argument there was no good reply. Tomson yielded, somewhat huffily no doubt, and tried to call the English troops back to their boats. A number of them responded dutifully. Others did not. "Some of our rude men, who make no account of friend or foe," Tomson reported, "fell to spoiling the Frenchmen, taking away their rings and jewels as from enemies; whereupon all the bulwarks and ports were turned against us."

The guns of the Calais fort opened up on the English boats, sending Tomson and everyone else—swordsmen and sailors and looters alike—scurrying for safety. The Spaniards managed to escape with their lives, but the guns did score a few hits. The *Margaret and John*, still stuck on her sandbar, was holed through twice before she could be floated off on the flood tide.

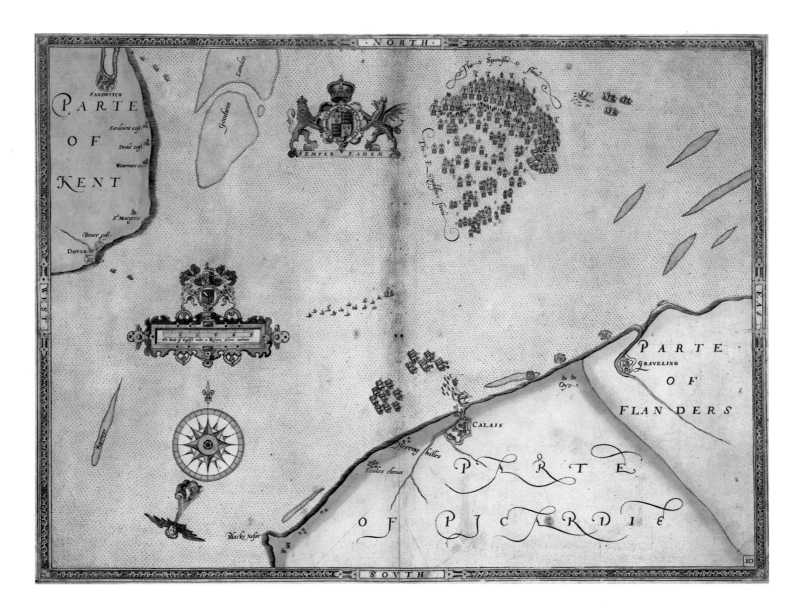

With the galleass now in the hands of the French, Lord Howard gathered his squadron together and hurried after the rest of the English fleet. He could hear the rolling broadsides of a much greater battle under way some dozen miles to the northeast, off the village of Gravelines. The sounds of war carried faint at first against the wind, then built to thunderous intensity as he drew nearer.

In all the surviving accounts of this epic 16th Century clash off the coast of Gravelines, there remains a frustrating uncertainty about what actually took place. No one bothered to make diagrams of fleet tactics, or even to make a record of individual ship movements with any precision. In the noise and smoke, the confusion bordered on outright chaos. With visibility ending at times at a vessel's own gunwale, it was often impossible to distinguish friend from foe, much less tell what everyone else was doing. From the diaries and statements of men who took part, only the general outline of the fighting—with flashes of surpassing gallantry and drama—shows clear. The battle raged on for nine hours, from sev-

At the entrance to Calais harbor, a squadron under Lord Howard finishes off the solitary galleass San Lorenzo as the rest of the English fleet pursues the hastily regrouping Armada past Gravelines, a few miles to the northeast of Calais.

en in the morning until four in the afternoon, and what seems to have happened was this.

As Drake led his squadron toward the fleeing Armada, Medina Sidonia and his four companion ships weighed anchor and steered north, away from the shore, in an attempt to intercept. The Duke's small band of galleons would stand fast against the oncoming English warships in a heroic delaying tactic, earning some time for the rest of the Armada to regroup. Pinnaces were already speeding up the coast to rally the scattered ships. Some of these ships had driven east as far as Dunkirk; they were hours away from the battlefront and in considerable danger of running up on the Flemish sands. The *San Martín* continued on her northern course for a while, gaining sea room—and gradually drifting apart from her companions. Suddenly she had to face the charge of Drake's *Revenge*.

As the *Revenge* boiled down toward the Spanish flagship, there was a drum roll, a ruffle of trumpets, then silence. The distance between the two ships slowly narrowed: to cannon range, to musket shot, then closer still—closer than any English ship had yet come to an Armada galleon. Still the *Revenge* bore soundlessly on, her gun crews poised over their weapons with smoking match, her musketeers and harque-

In the melee off Gravelines on August 8, 1588, Spanish seamen abandon a sinking galleon (foreground) while other vessels of the Armada flounder and burn under the onslaught of the English.

busiers braced against the bulwarks and in the mast tops. At perhaps 100 yards Drake gave the order to fire.

A spurt of flame and smoke erupted from the *Revenge's* bow guns. She luffed up to unleash a quick, splintering broadside, then swung back downwind and out of range. Directly behind came Thomas Fenner in the *Nonpareil*, swooping by the *San Martín* in an identical, point-blank flying assault. One by one the rest of the 20-odd ships in Drake's squadron sped past in their commander's wake, subjecting the Spanish flagship to a nonstop, gunwale-to-gunwale blitz of cannon fire. Then, as suddenly as it had come, the squadron disengaged. Having set the example for aggressive, close-up bombardment, Drake led his force downwind to challenge the ships to leeward.

The next squadron to reach the *San Martín* was Martin Frobisher's. Frobisher drew up beside the flagship, a pistol shot away, struck his topsails and stayed to pound her with his guns. The rest of his squadron swarmed about the Spanish galleon like hounds around a wounded boar, crossing her bow and stern, and nosing up from leeward to pummel her opposite side.

It seems miraculous that any vessel could have survived such a mauling. The *San Martín* was outnumbered by at least 10 to 1, and she was now holding at bay some of the strongest ships in Elizabeth's navy. She took 200 rounds in her starboard side alone, three of her guns were blasted off their mountings, her sails and rigging hung in tatters, and her decks lay strewn with dying men.

"The holes made in her hull between wind and water caused so great a leakage," declared the Armada's chief purser, Pedro Coco Calderón, "that two divers could hardly stop them up with hemp caulking and lead plates, working all day." But survive she did. As the flagship drifted eastward with the wind, the rest of her detachment worked their way back to her rescue, followed by the first returnees from the scattered fleet. Frobisher let her go and rejoined his own forces. The *San Martín* retired to patch her wounds. A few hours later she was back in the center of action.

While Frobisher was smothering the *San Martín* in great shot, Drake and his squadron sped northeast over the horizon, presumably to head off the returning Armada ships. No one knows his precise tactics. He left no report, other than to tell a chronicler how, in the heat of battle, the *Revenge* "was pierced with shot above forty times," and to describe how "his very cabben was twise shot thorow," and how "the bedde of a certaine gentleman lying weary thereupon was taken quite from under him with the force of a bullet." Drake loved a fine tale, and he may have empurpled his narrative with a few more gunshots and saber cuts than actually occurred. Still, he must have found the kind of roving dogfight he was best at. "The Prince of Parma and the Duke of Sidonia shall not shake hands this few days," he declared afterward with some smugness, "and whensoever they shall meet, I believe neither of them will greatly rejoice of this day's service."

Not even Drake could hold back the entire force of the Armada's fighting sail, however. Gradually the ragged squadrons regrouped, and hauled back to the main engagement off Gravelines. When John Haw-

This large drum, two feet in diameter, bears the coat of arms of Sir Francis Drake, who carried it into battles all over the world. Legend has it that should England ever be in danger again the drum's chilling tattoo will sound spontaneously, summoning Drake to the rescue.

Archers on the Ark Royal loose their arrows as English gunners exchange fire with a ship barely a pike's length away. Though a Spanish grapnel hovers menacingly over the Ark in this 19th Century engraving, the Spaniards never got close enough to use the dreaded hook.

kins reached the battle, he faced a grim cluster of top-line Spanish warships, the same powerful vessels that had borne the heat of the skirmishes in the English Channel: Juan Martínez de Recalde's *San Juan de Portugal*, Alonso de Leiva's *Rata Santa María Encoronada*, Miguel de Oquendo's *Santa Ana*, Martín de Bertendona's *Regazona*, and two crack Portuguese galleons, the *San Mateo* and the *San Felipe*, commanded by Diego de Pimentel and Francisco de Toledo respectively.

Bit by bit amid the roar and chaos, with a stubborn discipline that must have struck the English as positively uncanny, the Armada ships moved to recover their battle-tested defensive crescent. When William Wynter sailed up next with the Dover squadron, he saw, through the curtain of smoke, that the Armada had gone "into a proportion of a half moon. Their admiral and vice admiral, they went in the midst, and the greater number of them; and there went on each side, in the wings, their galleasses, armadas of Portugal, and other good ships, in the whole to the number of sixteen to a wing."

Wynter and his commander, Henry Seymour, charged down on the Armada's starboard wing. They aimed at the formation's weathermost tip, which was occupied by the Portuguese galleon *San Felipe*. The two

Englishmen held fire, as Drake had done, until the distance narrowed to about 100 yards. Musket and harquebus fire from the *San Felipe*'s mast tops and upper works splattered their decks. Seymour, in the lead, unloosed a broadside; Wynter followed with another. The two ships then crossed the *San Felipe*'s stern and rounded up under her lee. As other squadron members moved in close after them, the Portuguese galleon was encircled by a ring of 17 ships, according to one account, their guns spewing broadsides in a deadly, point-blank cross fire. "Out of my ship there was shot 500 shot of demi-cannon, culverin and demi-culverin," Wynter declared, "and when I was farthest off in discharging any of the pieces, I was not out of shot of their harquebus, and most time within speech of one another."

Close encounters of this sort were a departure for the English. Never in all the Channel skirmishes had they plunged so aggressively into the Spanish cluster. As the next Armada galleon, the *San Mateo*, luffed up to support the *San Felipe*, a detachment of Seymour's squadron broke off to assault her. She, too, was quickly encircled. One ship, skimming past the *San Mateo*'s rail, sailed so near that an English crewman leaped across to the galleon's deck—a one-man boarding party. Reckless heroism: He was instantly cut to bits. It was also unnecessary. As the English continued circling, guns blazing, the *San Mateo* began to crumble under their fire.

All along the battlefront, now, the English were moving in on the enemy, allowing just enough sea room to keep themselves clear of the grappling lines that, according to standard tactics, the Spaniards could be expected to throw out. As they drew closer the English kept up a steady barrage with their broadside guns. The effect was devastating. The Armada ships were riddled with shot, their hulls punctured, their masts splintered and their sails in shreds.

The English seemed to be taking very little punishment in return. One reason may have been that they were simply outshooting the enemy, as they had done throughout the previous week. English marksmen were famous all over the Continent, and their weapons represented the cutting edge of 16th Century naval gunnery. The English cannon were lashed into place on heavy sea trucks built of the finest English oak and elm, for example, whereas on some of the Armada ships the guns were mounted on ordinary field carriages. After each discharge the Spanish field carriages would skitter uncontrollably across the deck in a "boisterous reverse," like bucking horses. And there was an additional problem now. The Spaniards had not expected that they would have to engage in a gun battle with the English, and as a result they carried only a limited amount of round shot. This supply was now running out. One by one the great guns aboard the Armada galleons began falling silent. The Spanish response to the English broadsides became a pitiful rattle of small-arms fire.

Such was now the case aboard the beleaguered *San Felipe*. She was in a terrible state. Her shot lockers were empty. Five guns in her starboard broadside had been carried off their mounts. Her upper decks were a shambles of splintered planking and timber. Her hull leaked alarmingly, and both her pumps were broken. Nearly half her men lay dead or wounded. She was, said the purser Calderón, "almost a wreck."

For all that, the *San Felipe* did not stop fighting. Her commander, Francisco de Toledo, ordered out grapnels and challenged the closest English vessel—probably Seymour's *Rainbow*—to hand-to-hand combat. "They replied, summoning him to surrender in fair fight," Calderón wrote, "and one Englishman, standing in the maintop with his sword and buckler, called out, 'Good soldiers that ye are, surrender to the fair terms we offer ye.'

"The only answer he got was a gunshot, which brought him down in sight of everyone. And the commander then ordered the muskets and harquebuses into action. The enemy thereupon retired, while our men shouted out that they were cowards, abusing them for want of spirit, calling them Lutheran hens, and daring them to return to the fight."

With the odds running strong against them, the Spaniards were making a heroic stand. The fiercest action seemed to be concentrated on the Armada's right flank, where other galleons had turned back to succor the *San Felipe* and her equally battered sister ship, the *San Mateo*. Recalde arrived in the *San Juan de Portugal* to take on "10 of the enemy's greatships," said Calderón. Bertendona's great carrack, the *Regazona*, was seen wallowing past, her big guns silenced and blood pouring through her scuppers, but with musketeers still clinging to her tops, ready to fight again. Medina Sidonia had heard the sharp crackle of musketry on his right flank, and tried to find out what was happening. Unable to see through the billowing miasma that surrounded the ships, he ordered the helmsman to steer back to help. He found the *San Mateo* in such sorry condition—"riddled with shot like a sieve"—that he dispatched boats to bring off her soldiers and crew. Her commander, Diego de Pimentel, asked instead for a diver to repair his leaks. He refused to leave his quarter-deck.

High gallantry, but it could not last forever. Outgunned and outnumbered—Lord Howard had caught up with the battle after his morning diversion at Calais—the besieged Armada galleons began to fall back. With their ammunition gone, and with the wind and current pushing the entire battlefront eastward, in the direction of the Flanders sandbanks, the time had come to look for an escape route.

The opportunity to break off arrived at around four in the afternoon, in the form of a violent rain squall. The sky blackened in the west, a sudden front moved in, and in the shock of wind and lashing rain, all fighting ceased. For the next quarter hour or so each captain had all he could handle to try to bring his flogging sails and bucking helm under control. Then, as the gusts began to subside, the Spaniards were able to bear off to the northeast, ahead of the English and into the open water of the North Sea.

The English let them go. They, too, were running low on ammunition and were ready to quit. Howard gathered his squadrons and took stock of the damage. There was remarkably little. A few ships had been holed, but none sunk. The English casualties, counting the men killed at Calais, numbered perhaps 100 dead.

Clearly the English had achieved a major success. They had fractured the powerful Armada crescent, after a week of unsuccessful trying. They had prevented the rendezvous with Parma—at least temporarily. The English gunners had scored heavily. The two Portuguese galleons, the *San Felipe* and the *San Mateo*, could be seen riding dangerously low in the water. As sunset approached, the *María Juan*, a large Biscayan galleon that was drifting between the two fleets, sank to the bottom, taking 275 men along with her.

Lord Admiral Howard could see that more would have to be done, however. Even as he looked on, the surviving vessels of the Armada proceeded to reassemble themselves into their stubborn, menacing half-moon. The Battle of Gravelines was something less than the triumphant rout that the Lord Admiral had wanted. That night he wrote an urgent note to Walsingham asking him to send more powder, more shot, more victuals, for "their force is wonderful great and strong; and yet we pluck their feathers little by little."

Two more feathers dropped later that night. The *San Felipe* was one.

Declaring the piety of the Armada's mission, this crucifixion scene adorned a linen banner taken from the disabled San Mateo after the battle of Gravelines. A 16th Century warship might carry more than two dozen different flags; the nation, the monarch, the Church, the commander, the squadron, and even the nobles who were aboard claimed the right to display their colors.

When it became obvious that she was going to sink, Francisco de Toledo fired a signal cannon to summon aid. One of the urcas drew alongside, and everyone transferred over to it. Then somehow a rumor started that the urca also was sinking. Toledo, along with the ship's captain and some of the crew, leaped back aboard the *San Felipe*—as if drowning in a galleon was more dignified than drowning in a hulk. By the time he learned his mistake, it was too late. The seas were rising and the urca was forced to bear away.

Toledo took the only course that was left open to him—he drove the *San Felipe* east toward Flanders. She ran aground on the sands somewhere between Ostend and Nieuport, where patrolling Dutchmen came across her the next morning. Townspeople from Nieuport soon arrived on the scene in pinnaces. They sacked the ship and then towed her off to Flushing. No record survives of how they dealt with Toledo, his officers and his crew.

As for the *San Mateo*, she staggered along with the fleet through most of the night, her pumps laboring to keep out the water. It was no use. A short while after sunrise she turned toward the Flanders coast and fetched up on the sands between Ostend and Sluys. Three Dutch flyboats swooped down to pick up the pieces. Diego de Pimentel and his men fought them off for a full two hours, before surrendering. Pimentel was held for ransom, along with the various other notables aboard. The crewmen and common soldiers were cast over the side to drown. Not long afterward a great ship's banner—probably from the *San Mateo*—was carried in triumph to the Protestant cathedral at Leiden, where it was hung in display from the vault. Its length was so great that the fringe reached all the way to the pavement.

Most of the other top-line Armada galleons were in scarcely better condition. The *San Marcos*, which had fought steadily since early morning, was so battered that three heavy cables had to be wound around her hull to keep it from splitting apart. The Armada had suffered heavy casualties—600 dead and 800 wounded by official tally, many more in certain fact. Yet the Spaniards had no intention of giving up. Medina Sidonia declared himself ready to turn about-face and meet the enemy again if necessary—and, in spite of all the obstacles facing him, to make his rendezvous with Parma.

But as dawn broke on Tuesday, August 9, he must have known how impossible this would be. During the night the wind had intensified and shifted into the northwest. The fleet, with many ships barely manageable because of broken spars and shredded sails, was being driven inexorably before it. The Duke was sailing in the rear, and looking back over the taffrail he could watch the English fleet trailing after him, a mile or two to windward. However, the real danger lay in the opposite direction, to leeward. Beyond his starboard bow the roll of the sea was changing to a short, menacing chop. Farther on it was breaking into an endless line of white froth. The Armada was being driven onto the Flanders sandbanks. After years of planning and preparation, after the millions of ducats invested, after quantities of blood spent and uncounted agonies endured, the Enterprise of England seemed about to smash itself to pieces on a Flemish beach.

Bearing the words "I blow and
scatter" in Latin, a wind from the heavens
drives the Armada away from the
coast of England. The Dutch engraver of
this scene underscored his belief in
the divine determination of the outcome
with the Latin inscription "The right
hand of God makes prosperity."

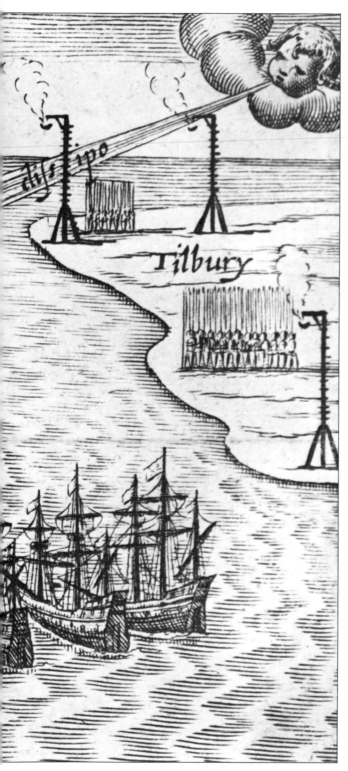

There was no escape, the Duke's pilots said, no way of clawing back against that wind and these heavy seas. The fleet was caught in the mariner's most dreaded predicament—with crippled ships, in a storm, against a foul lee shore. "We saw ourselves lost or taken by the enemy," moaned an aide aboard the flagship, "or the whole Armada drowned upon the banks. It was the most fearful day in the world." Miguel de Oquendo came by in the *Santa Ana*, and the Duke hailed him.

"Señor Oquendo, what shall we do?" he asked. "We are lost!"

"Ask Diego Flores," Oquendo called back, taking a contemptuous gibe at the Duke's hated chief adviser. "As for me, I am going to fight, and die like a man. Send me a supply of shot."

Death in battle seemed preferable to an inglorious drowning—although there was hardly any shot left to fight with, of course. Medina Sidonia luffed up, shortened sail and let go his anchor. The other rearguard vessels did the same. The drift to leeward slowed, but not enough. With the force of wind and sea the ships continued dragging toward the banks. The leadsmen in the bow called soundings: seven fathoms, then six. The *San Martín* drew five. Medina Sidonia summoned his priest and knelt down on the poop deck to make his last confession. And to pray for a miracle.

At a distance of perhaps two miles, Lord Howard had been trailing the Armada, and he knew exactly what kind of peril it faced. His own galleons, even deeper drafted than the Spanish ones, had kept just enough sea room themselves to stay clear of the shallows. Howard had no intention of joining the enemy in a death-or-victory melee upon the sands. There was no need for it, he reasoned. When the Armada's rear guard turned back to face him, he also luffed up—and waited. The wind could complete the work of destruction.

Suddenly, with surprising nimbleness, the wind shifted. It backed some 80° around the compass into west-southwest. As Howard stood by in astonishment, the Armada ships raised anchor, bent on sail, and moved away from the coast into the clear, open reaches of the North Sea. The miracle had occurred.

There was nothing Howard could do but move after them. He detached Lord Seymour to resume the watch on Parma—much to the outraged protests of Seymour himself, who after his derring-do at Gravelines felt entitled to a place at the kill. Then, as the Lord Admiral reported to Walsingham, "notwithstanding that our powder and shot was well near all spent, we set on a bragging countenance and gave them chase."

The English sailed northward in the wake of the retreating Spanish vessels—past Margate and Harwich, up past Yarmouth and Hull, beyond Newcastle in Northumberland, and on past the Scottish border. By Friday, the 12th of August, their provisions were nearly exhausted. Howard broke off the pursuit and, after putting in at the Firth of Forth for food and water, steered for home. He did so with misgivings, however, for in the back of his mind there lingered a nagging apprehension that—despite all odds and in the face of reason itself—the Spanish fleet at any moment might reverse its flight, swing back and resume its assault on England's sovereign realm.

Enduring images of a nation's triumph

While the experience of the Armada was still fresh in his mind, Lord Howard of Effingham, the admiral who had led the English to victory, began to amass a pictorial record of the great naval encounter. The documentation itself became an epic enterprise: Howard oversaw the making of diagrams, charts, maps, drawings, paintings and—that most medieval of art forms—tapestries.

Of all the renditions, the most spectacular were the tapestries: 10 gigantic wall hangings that measured from 19 to 29 feet in width, and 15 feet from floor to ceiling. Under Howard's direction, the two Dutch artists who made them (Hendrick Corneliszoom Vroom of Haarlem did the designs, François Spierincx of Delft the weaving) re-created the smoke and tumult of the entire engagement in such rich detail that every important move of the battle could be followed, from the stately beginnings to the chaotic close. On each tapestry, the royal arms of England were suspended above the field of action, and portraits of the leading commanders appeared in the borders. Howard himself occupied the central position along the top edge (below).

For about a quarter of a century, the tapestries hung in Howard's palatial London residence. But the great naval hero who had managed to keep the Spaniards off English soil proved unable to keep his own accounts in order; in 1616 he had to sell the tapestries to pay personal debts. The buyer was Queen Elizabeth's successor, King James I, who put them on permanent display in the House of Lords.

In the 18th Century they caught the eye of an enterprising engraver by the name of John Pine. Worrying patriotically that "Time, or Accident, or Moths may deface these valuable Shadows" (and no doubt envisioning handsome profits for himself), he undertook to copy the entire tapestry sequence. His prints, with the images reduced to a scale of about an inch to the foot, appeared in 1739.

Pine's fears for the tapestries were entirely justified. On October 16, 1834, workmen in the cellar of the House of Lords stoked the furnace with too much wood. Flames swept through Westminster Palace, and the 10 tapestries were destroyed. Fortunately, the engraved replications have endured. Seven of them are reproduced here and on the following pages, all (except the one below) minus only their borders, and each accompanied by an enlarged detail.

Off Lizard Point at the head of the English Channel, the Armada falls into formation for its advance on the coast of England.

Having maneuvered the English fleet around and behind the horns of the Armada crescent (left), Lord Howard of Effingham opens the Channel fighting in almost courtly fashion by sending one of his pinnaces ahead to discharge a round at the Spanish flagship.

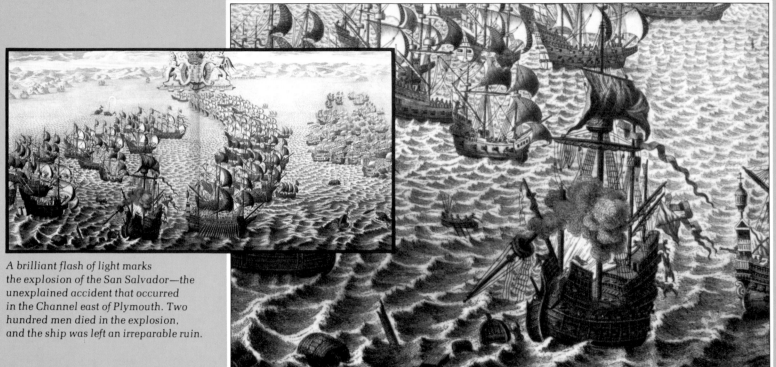

A brilliant flash of light marks
the explosion of the San Salvador—the
unexplained accident that occurred
in the Channel east of Plymouth. Two
hundred men died in the explosion,
and the ship was left an irreparable ruin.

Three English ships—the Ark Royal,
the White Bear and the Mary Rose—stray
perilously close to the rear of the
Armada crescent, while Sir Francis Drake
in the Revenge conducts a private
assault on the dismasted carrack Nuestra
Señora del Rosario (detail, below).

As Spanish galleasses row into position for battle in a dead calm off the Isle of Wight, longboats begin to swing the English galleons around to deliver a devastating blast of their own.

Belching flames and smoke, eight English fire ships bear down upon the Armada at an anchorage off the port of Calais, causing the Spaniards to cut their cables and scatter in confusion.

As the confrontation in the Channel draws to its close, the disabled Spanish galleass San Lorenzo founders on a sandbar off Calais and English longboats move in for the kill. Meanwhile, the English warships pursue the fleeing Armada into the North Sea (left).

Chapter 6

The winds of God

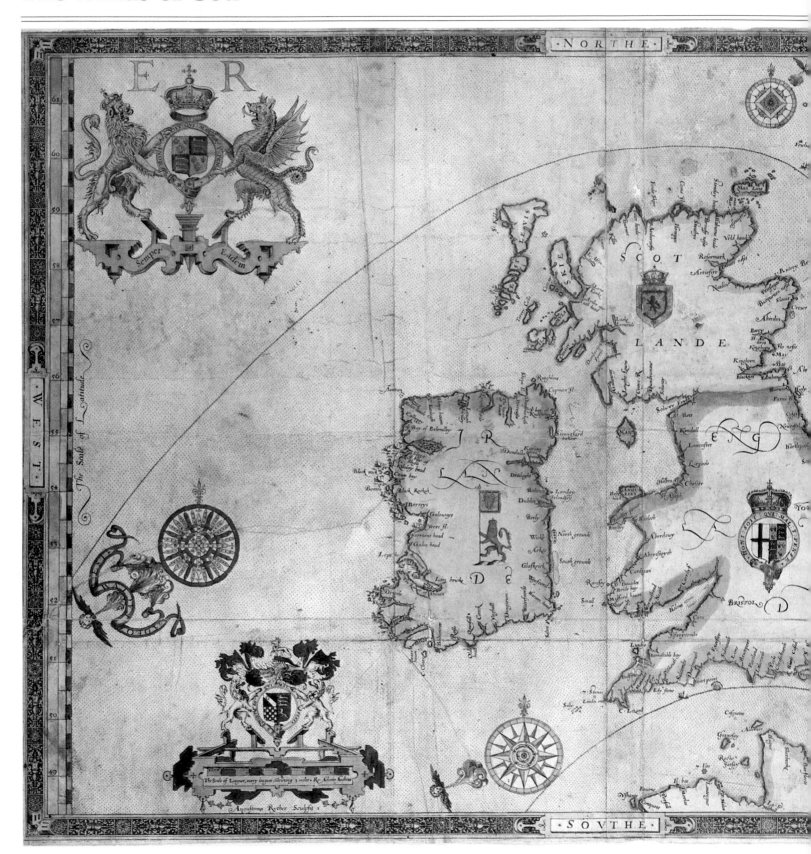

In a map-narration of the Armada campaign's conclusion, the
Spanish ships flee around the British Isles—more than 20 of them
ending in wreckage on the shores of Scotland and Ireland.

he ships of the Spanish Armada had fought four battles with the English—but who had won? And what was next? The answers to these questions were not entirely clear at first. Preliminary reports on the Continent gave victory to the Spaniards. In France, rumors spread that the English had lost 15 warships; that a galleass had attacked Drake's *Revenge,* brought down all her masts with one broadside and sunk her with the next; that Drake had fled the field in abject terror in a small boat. When this story proved to be false, it was supplanted by another, this one saying that after the encounter off Gravelines there had been one more battle, farther to the north, in which the English had suffered a painful bruising; that the *Ark Royal* had been blasted to smithereens and that John Hawkins had been sent to the bottom; that Drake had assailed the *San Martín,* attempted to board her, and been cut to pieces. A variation on this tale had it that Drake's leg had been shot away and that he was being held prisoner; that scores of English ships had been sunk, and the others had retreated in panic; that the Armada had made a landing in Scotland and now was returning to rendezvous with Parma.

On the strength of these stories the Spanish Ambassador in Paris lit a bonfire in front of his embassy. In Rome, Philip's emissary marched into the Vatican to suggest that triumphal Masses be said throughout Christendom, and to demand the million gold ducats promised by the Pope for a successful invasion.

King Philip listened to the reports with prim equanimity, mulling them over in his austere chambers at El Escorial. A celebration, he pointed out, would be premature. For he had heard other accounts, less encouraging than these, of Spanish ships captured and sunk. He decided that it would be preferable to wait until a final reckoning could be obtained.

The English, despite their proximity to the field of battle, were no more certain of the outcome than anyone else. And unanswered questions still remained. Why had no Spanish ships been boarded and captured? the Queen wanted to know. Where were the vast numbers of prisoners that should have been taken? Where were the treasure chests of Spanish gold? And why was Lord Howard using up so much expensive powder and shot? "Our half-doings doth breed dishonor and leaveth the disease uncured," grumbled her Principal Secretary, Francis Walsingham. Queen Elizabeth and her counselors simply did not understand the tactics of massive bombardment that had sent the Armada fleeing.

That the Spaniards were gone, at least for the moment, was beyond doubt. Dispatches from Howard, Drake and others told of the pursuit northward to Scotland, and the Queen could take satisfaction in their estimates that seven Spanish ships had been battered. No one guessed how severely battered, though. And no one knew what the Armada would do next. Some people expected that the fleet would make for Hamburg; the Spaniards undoubtedly needed extensive repairs and quick transfusions of water and provisions, and Hamburg was a friendly port that had already supplied a few vessels to the Enterprise of England.

Drake believed that Denmark would be an even likelier place for the Spaniards to turn for help. The Danish King "is a prince of great shipping," Drake explained to Walsingham, "and what the King of Spain's hot crowns will do in cold countries for mariners and men, I leave to your Lordship." Howard believed that the fleet might try to sail around Ireland and head south into the Atlantic and back to Spain. Unless, of course, the Spaniards decided to come about, return to the Channel and resume the fight.

Another unpleasant possibility remained. Perhaps the Spanish retreat was only a feint, intended to lure the English fleet north and clear the Channel of its defenses—thus opening a passage for Parma's invasion forces, which were still poised menacingly in Flanders. That thought worried Drake even as he romped north in eager pursuit of the enemy. He sent London a word of caution: "Have a good eye to the Duke of Parma." A few days later, having scudded back to port on the tail of a three-day storm, he repeated his warning: "As to the Duke of Parma, I take him to be as a bear robbed of her whelps!"

London did not have to be told. Ever since the arrival of the Armada in the English Channel, the townspeople had been preparing for the expected assault. Heavy iron chains were hung across the city's streets to barricade them, armed volunteers patrolled day and night, and officials at Westminster cast about for recruits to stiffen the Queen's sorely understaffed bodyguard.

The principal defense force was stationed at Tilbury, on the north bank of the Thames River, approximately 20 miles to the east of London. Somewhere between 10,000 and 20,000 men—no records survive to give the exact figure—had been hastily gathered under the command of the 56-year-old Earl of Leicester, Queen Elizabeth's earliest court favorite and now her captain general. During the fighting in the Channel, Leicester had been working feverishly to set up camp, to assemble pikemen and horsemen, and to bring in arms, provisions and beer—all of which were essential for a proper defense and exasperatingly slow to arrive. The earl appeared to be doing the job singlehandedly. "I am here to cook, cater and hunt," he complained to Walsingham. But after a while, the encampment began to take shape. Ditches were dug, palisades erected, multicolored pavilions set up for the noblemen and officers, and green tents for those of lesser rank. By the time the first reports trickled back from Gravelines, the camp stood as ready to meet Parma's invasion as it ever would. A period of spring tides was approaching—the most favorable time for a launching of troop barges—and on the morning of Thursday, August 18, Queen Elizabeth set out from St. James's Palace in London to inspect the troops.

The Queen arrived by royal barge, and she lodged at a nearby inn for two days. The first afternoon she rode out to camp to make an inspection. An attendant nobleman led the way, carrying the Sword of State. Behind him came two pages wearing white velvet. Then came Elizabeth, mounted on a snow-white palfrey, the white-haired Earl of Leicester posting at her right hand and the darkly handsome Earl of Essex, her current favorite, at her left. She was clad from neck to toe in

Mounted on a white palfrey, Queen Elizabeth rides to Tilbury to review the English land forces as the Armada burns symbolically in the background; in the upper scene she sits with an open Bible, thanking God for victory. The picture, part of an altar diptych, is painted on wood believed to have been scavenged from a Spanish wreck.

white velvet, an embossed silver cuirass guarding her bosom, her auburn wig caught up in a sizzle of diamonds and pearls and plumes, and as she moved among the regiments she seemed to glow with a courageous and majestic benevolence. The effect was extraordinary. Cheer upon cheer burst from the ranks and rolled out across the encampment, a thundering babel of endearment and praise. This was their own Virgin Queen, Gloriana herself at the apogee of her reign, embracing her people in their finest hour.

Elizabeth liked the experience so much that she repeated it the following day. This time she delivered a speech, as fine and stirring in its grand Shakespearean cadences as any spoken by an English monarch: "I am come amongst you as you see, at this time, not for my recreation and disport, but being resolved, in the midst and heat of the battle, to live or die amongst you all; and to lay down for my God, for my kingdom and for my people, my honor and my blood, even in the dust," she said, adding: "I have the heart and stomach of a King, and of a King of England too." Then, after hurling scorn at Parma and his monarch for daring to invade her realm, she concluded stirringly: "I myself will be your General, Judge, and Rewarder of every one of your virtues in the field."

What an awesome performance! The Queen seemed truly determined to remain at Tilbury, astride her white palfrey, and drive her ceremonial sword into the breast of the first Spanish trooper to step ashore. With considerable difficulty her advisers hustled her away from the front line and back to St. James's.

There were other matters that demanded her urgent attention—not the least of which was the sorry condition of the royal navy. Lord Howard's ships had been at sea, in heavy combat, for nearly three uninterrupted weeks. By the time they straggled back to Harwich, Margate and the various other havens near the mouth of the Thames, they were badly deteriorated—not so much from Spanish shot as from the sea itself. Ship after ship exhibited strained timbers, leaky planking, and worn and broken rigging. The *Triumph* had developed dry rot in her bow and forecastle, and two of her beams were cracked. Hawkins' *Victory* was "in great decay," and so was Lord Sheffield's *White Bear*. Every ship required fumigating, scraping and recalking before it could be returned to service.

The mariners themselves were even worse off. The fleet had put to sea in a hurry, without sufficient victuals, and by now the stores of bacon, biscuit and fresh water were almost exhausted. The few remaining rations had begun to putrefy. The men were "driven to such extremity for lack of meat," according to one report, "that my Lord Admiral was driven to eat beans, and some to drink their own water." Shocking measures both—if both indeed were taken. Then also, those attendant evils of shipboard life—dysentery and typhus—were exacting a dreadful toll. Almost half of the *White Bear's* 500 crewmen had been overcome, and infection was rife aboard most of the other vessels. "Mortality begins wonderfully to grow amongst us," Lord Howard reported to Burghley from Margate. And from Dover he informed the Queen: "They sicken one day and die the next."

Pennies put by against the future

For all the misery they inflict, wars frequently activate humanitarian impulses as well. A compassionate legacy of the English clash with the Armada was the Chatham Chest—a fund for "poor sailors maimed in the navy," and one of the earliest instances of government-sponsored workmen's compensation.

The driving force behind the fund was Sir John Hawkins, who was as untiring in his concern for the welfare of his men as for the fighting prowess of English ships. In 1590, in collaboration with Lord Howard and Sir Francis Drake, he began the collection of sixpence per month from seamen's wages, to be saved for future compensation payments. The coins were kept in a chest at the royal dockyards in Chatham.

This repository of wealth proved too tempting for dockyard workers, and the chest was pilfered repeatedly. In response, the Admiralty transferred the money to a sturdier chest (below), secured it with five locks, and gave the keys to various officers appointed by the Admiralty; the chest could be opened only when all its guardians were present. Unfortunately, the guardians sometimes tapped the till to make private investments.

Despite thefts and embezzlement, the fund served its intended purpose for the most part, supplying pensions to the needy, providing lump-sum compensation for various injuries (a severe bruise received in the line of duty brought two pounds) and paying for the burial of veteran seamen. The Chatham Chest survived as a national institution until 1814, when it was merged with the even grander scheme of the Greenwich Hospital Fund, which not only dispensed alms to disabled seamen but also provided bed and board.

This 1625 version of the Chatham Chest, made of cast iron, was three feet long and two and one half feet deep.

No one knew what was causing the epidemic, or what to do about it. The blame was attributed, variously, to something in the pitch used for calking, and to sour beer. The correct explanation—the appalling filth and crowding of life at sea—did not occur to anyone. An obvious remedy was to disembark the men, but this could not be accomplished all at once. Shore facilities were simply too limited to accommodate thousands of demobilized sailors. Furthermore, no one had the necessary money to pay them off. Howard drummed Westminster with pleas for funds to feed and discharge the men. But for weeks the stricken crew languished on the ships, in sight of port, while the royal bureaucracy tried to squeeze the necessary sterling out of the war-depleted treasury.

In the end the Lord Admiral paid off as many of the men as he could out of his own pocket. "Before God, I would rather have never a penny in the world than they should lack," he declared. It was not possible for him to take care of everyone, however. The demobilized crews staggered ashore, sick, hungry and broke, and in such numbers that many lay dying in the streets from sheer neglect. No wonder, then, that the men who had fought so valiantly, and sent the Armada fleeing northward, felt no sense of triumph.

Aboard the ships of the Spanish fleet, there was no question who had won. Spanish officers and men could clearly see that their once-proud Armada had been blasted almost beyond recognition. Of the 130 vessels that had sailed so majestically from Lisbon more than three months before, scarcely 100 remained; the rest were captured, sunk or lost at sea. Many of the survivors were so ravaged by shot that they could barely stay afloat, and most were short of food and drink. Hundreds of water barrels, stowed on deck, had been pierced by shot. The stores of salt beef, cheese and tuna had been moldering away week after week in their green-wood casks, until they had turned inedible. Thousands of sick and wounded men lay dying belowdecks.

Even so, the Spaniards had not yet lost heart. The day after the confrontation at Gravelines, as the fleet ran north with the English on its tail, Medina Sidonia gathered his chief officers in conference to assess the situation and to take a vote. Astonishingly, the men voted that, should the wind turn fair, the fleet would reverse direction, head back toward Flanders and, despite its losses, make one last attempt to complete its mission—the rendezvous with Parma.

This decided, Medina Sidonia took steps to restore discipline. In order to prevent a recurrence of incidents like the one at Calais, where the fleet had ignored his signal to stick together in the face of the English fireboats, Medina Sidonia conducted a court-martial in which 20 delinquent captains were sentenced to be hanged. Nineteen of these were granted reprieves—perhaps because the Duke could not afford to reduce his staff by so large a number—but one unfortunate man was swung from the yardarm of a pinnace and paraded through the fleet as a grim warning and example to the rest. Then the Duke, who had scarcely left his quarter-deck these past two weeks, retired to his cabin in a state of collapse.

A desperate race to stay afloat

After a full week's furious bombardment by the ship-killing guns of the English, the frontline vessels of the Armada were so battered and torn that many were barely recognizable. The flagship *San Martín* alone had taken at least 500 cannon balls in her hull and rigging, and almost every other surviving ship had suffered one kind of injury or another. It was grimly obvious to the Spanish commanders that, no matter whether the future held more fighting or a run for home, the fleet would have to spend some time on repairs.

Fortunately, the Spaniards had the wherewithal to do the most urgent work at sea. Every vessel carried along extra spars and rope, lumber for planking, bolts of canvas, quantities of oxhides and lead sheets to cover gaping holes, and barrels of tar and oakum to calk opened seams. Ships even brought along cloth patterns that could be used to ensure the proper shaping of a new rudder—the most vital part of all. As for craftsmen, each vessel carried carpenters, sail-makers, coopers, blacksmiths—and sometimes armorers,

who had enlisted to service the forces that had been expected to make the land invasion.

As the crippled Spanish fleet limped away from Gravelines and into the North Sea—still in sight of English scouting vessels—the ships' companies set about dealing with the damage inflicted by the foe. The first order of business was to stanch the leaking: Soldiers joined the sailors in manning the bilge pumps through all watches, while the more experienced seamen labored to patch up the worst of the holes and restore a measure of structural soundness to shot-weakened hulls. Once a vessel was out of danger of sinking, the men turned their attention to splintered masts, shredded rigging, tattered sails, and a host of other injuries. Considering the plight of the fleet, their efforts—pictured here and on the following pages—were remarkably successful: Of the 100 or so ships that managed to reach the North Sea after the battle of Gravelines, only three succumbed to their wounds.

Spanish sailors stand in a ship's boat beneath the stern gallery of a listing galleon to inspect damage to her rudder and to patch gunshot holes in the transom. On the galleon's deck, other sailors begin to slash away the useless rigging of the wrecked foremast, whose flinders lie floating off the port bow, while a third group of seamen tries to lower the shredded main-topsail.

Standing on a makeshift stage of wooden planks, two ship's carpenters pound wooden plugs into the holes in the battered galleon's topsides. Above them a group of sailors measure a timber to use as a section of railing, while a lone sailor, suspended in a bosun's chair, saws off jagged splinters from the stump of the foremast. In the water, several divers begin making repairs on the underwater sections of the ship.

As a fellow diver goes up for air, two men nail a sheet of lead over a heavy wad of hempen fiber, called tow, that they have stuffed into a shot hole. To keep themselves from drifting away from their work, the divers carry small sacks of lead weights and wrap their arms around lines slung under the ship.

From stations on both sides of the beakhead, sailors pay out a hawser that will be cinched around the weakened hull. Other crewmen, taking advantage of the vessel's forward drift, hold lengths of smaller line tied to the hawser and haul it aft to the waist, where the cinching will be completed. On the forecastle deck, the white-hatted boatswain shouts orders to riggers raising a jury mast by means of a block and tackle suspended from the fork of two lashed timbers.

Two sailors lever a capstan bar sideways to tighten the lashings for the replacement mast, and a third seaman seizes them together with a handspike and a second line. Above them, a rigger secures one end of an improvised mast stay to the new spar—the first step in providing it with enough support to fly a small square sail.

Three sailors heave down on a capstan bar to wind tension into a loop of seizing line secured to the ends of the cinching. When the bar has been pulled down as far as it will go, the kneeling sailor will slide a second capstan bar into the gap in the twisted line—kept open by a small block of wood—so that his comrades can force the seizing loop even tighter. At the rail, carpenters begin to repair the galleon's bulwarks and gunports.

In the waist, a new rudder (center) and sternpost (right) are fashioned under the supervision of the pilot and the ship's carpenter, who holds a cloth pattern used as a guide in the cutting of replacement parts. At the forge (left) the blacksmith, aided by two shipboys, makes iron bolts, pintles and gudgeons that will be used to mount the jury rudder on the sternpost.

With numerous blocks and tackles, sailors lower the replacement rudder and sternpost onto the transom. A small cannon, temporarily lashed to the after edge of the rudder, will counteract its buoyancy and enable the sailors to fix it in place. Then, four bundles of chain, attached to the sternpost, will be untied and used to secure the rudder assembly to the galleon.

ventually, the wind off Scotland did change. It boiled up in "a mighty tempest," said a chronicler, and sent the Spaniards tumbling before it. The winds blew from August 13 to 18, leaving rain, fog and heavy seas in their wake. "It was impossible to distinguish one ship from another," observed the purser Pedro Coco Calderón, while riding in a gray swirl aboard the supply urca *San Salvador*. A well-found fleet would have weathered the storm without severe hardship or loss—as did the English, who had broken off their chase and ridden the winds back to port. For the Spaniards, whose nearest port lay some 2,000 miles away, the storm would prove fatal.

By the time the winds had finally blown themselves out, it had become evident to the Spaniards that the Enterprise of England was finished. "The Armada was so completely crippled and scattered," Medina Sidonia wrote Philip on August 21, "that my first duty to your Majesty was to save it." Some days earlier, the Armada pilots had worked out a contingency plan that called for sailing around Scotland and Ireland, then south through the Atlantic and so back to Spain. The plan was now put into effect.

To stretch the food and water as far as possible, emergency measures were ordered. The stable of mules and horses was driven overboard and left thrashing among the billows. Seamen and officers alike were put on half rations: half a pound of biscuit, a pint of water and half a pint of wine a day—barely enough to sustain life. Only the sick, who now numbered some 3,000 men, were exempt from this regimen; they were given special rations drawn from a reserve stock of rice meant for just such an emergency. Then, as he set the Armada's course north around Scotland, the admiral placed his trust in heaven. "God send us fair weather, so that we may soon reach port," he prayed, "for upon that depend the salvation of this army and navy."

He prayed in vain. As the Armada turned west toward Ireland and August gave way to September, a continued succession of fogs, squalls, head winds and early autumn blows descended. "We sailed without knowing whither, through constant storms," declared Calderón. Many of the ships had been so severely strained that they could not beat to windward without fear of opening their seams. Many could not head up at all. In the rare periods of clarity and calm, he remembered, he could see individual vessels fall behind, then vanish below the horizon. Day by day the ships were driven farther apart, until the Armada ceased to be a fleet, but became instead a straggle of isolated vagabonds, each striving to reach home before it sank or its men starved.

One of the first casualties was a 600-ton urca, the *Bark of Hamburg*. She had been leaking badly all along, and on September 1, somewhere north of Ireland, her pumps clogged and she began to founder. Her 264 crewmen were taken off by two other nearby vessels—the *Trinidad Valencera*, a huge Venetian argosy that had sailed with the Levant squadron, and the urca flagship *Gran Grifón*.

Their apparent salvation was pitifully short-lived. The *Trinidad Valencera* had been so severely weakened by cannon shot at Gravelines that now, as she bucked the head winds off the coast of Ireland, a major leak opened in her bows. On September 12, to keep afloat, she was forced to reverse her course and run in search of land. For two days she fled eastward, carrying more than seven feet of water sloshing in her hold, until she reached Malin Head, the northernmost point on the remote and rugged Irish coast. A flat, open bay stretched east of Malin Head, and as the *Trinidad Valencera* slid along it, looking for an anchorage, she ran hard against a reef.

Perhaps 600 men were aboard. Most of them managed to reach shore, either swimming or rowing in longboats, but 40 drowned. The survivors headed inland, hoping to find shelter among the Irish, who—as Catholics—sympathized with Spain. They found instead a battalion of English soldiers from the local garrison. Most of the Spanish officers were taken prisoner and held for ransom. Some 300 of the men were stripped naked, herded into a field and massacred. The remainder fled into the bogs, finding refuge among the Irish clans if they could. Only a handful ever made it back to Spain.

The story of the *Gran Grifón* is only slightly less dismal. The urca flagship was also taking on water as a result of the drubbing Drake had given her in the Channel four weeks before. After picking up the *Bark of Hamburg's* survivors, she had tried to head southwest into the Atlantic. The same blustery head winds that had turned back the *Trinidad Valencera* now hit her face-on. Her seams opened, some of them as much as a handbreadth apart, and she, like the *Valencera*, was compelled to head for the nearest shore.

After three days the wind shifted, and the urca put about for Spain. The crew patched her leaks with oxhide and planking, and steered her south along the west coast of Ireland. Around the latitude of Galway Bay another storm hit. Again the urca was forced to north, until the winds abated and she could turn back on course. On September 13 she was hit by yet another fury of wind and sea. She caromed north once more, wallowing and plunging for another three days in weather so fierce that the oxhide repairs were carried away. At dusk on the 26th, the *Gran Grifón* found herself dodging islands in the Orkneys, off northern Scotland. "During the night we gave ourselves up for lost, for the seas ran mountains high, and the rain fell in torrents," one survivor recalled. "Our two companies—230 men in all, and 40 we had taken from the other ship—pumped incessantly, and bailed with buckets, but the water still increased."

Somehow the *Gran Grifón* stayed afloat, conning her way through the islands by the light of intermittent lightning flashes, and the next day she fetched up at Fair Isle between the Orkneys and the Shetlands. Seventeen Scottish families lived on Fair Isle, in primitive thatched huts, and they harbored the refugees until a boat was found to carry them to the mainland. The Spaniards were taken to Edinburgh, the capital, and there they stayed, awaiting repatriation, while the officials of three nations deliberated over who should pay for their care and transport. A year passed before the matter was settled; finally the Duke of Parma himself chartered four Scottish merchantmen to carry the men back to Spain. Those particular Spaniards were extraordinarily lucky.

At least one other Armada vessel left her keel in Scotland. She was the

DRAVN AFTER · THE · QVICKE

San Juan de Sicilia, an 800-ton armed merchantman of the Levant squadron, and sometime during the storm of September 13 she dropped anchor in Tobermory Bay in Argyll. She swung on her cable for several weeks in apparent security until Francis Walsingham, back in London, learned of her presence. Walsingham sent a secret agent to Tobermory on a bold and savage mission. The agent somehow talked his way aboard and, he reported, "cast in the powder-room a piece of lint" to which he had applied a match—and then ran for his life. The resulting explosion blew the merchantman sky-high, killing almost all her 340 soldiers and crew.

By far the most disastrous Armada shipwrecks occurred on the desolate west coast of Ireland. The shoreline that runs south for 200 miles from Bloody Foreland in Donegal to the hidden rocks of Dingle Bay in Kerry is one of the most awesomely treacherous in the world, a jagged chaos of sudden reefs, swirling currents, deceptive inlets and stone abutments—some 1,000 feet high—that drop so sharply into the sea that they might have been sliced off by a giant cleaver. In the 16th Century it was all but uncharted. It took a chilling toll. During 10 fateful days, from September 16 to 26, at least 20 vessels struck the coastal cliff and shoal and shingle. On one beach in Sligo Bay near Donegal, a witness counted

In an anonymous 16th Century woodcut inscribed "drawn after the quicke" —that is, from life—two quarreling Irish warriors brandish their swords as four companions watch. "The Irish professed to be Christians," wrote a Spaniard who survived a shipwreck on the country's rocky coast, "but they were a wild, lawless race, and everyone did as he liked."

more than 1,200 cadavers washed up by the surf, along with immense piles of wreckage. No one knows how many Armada members perished in all; perhaps 4,000. For centuries afterward the waves washed sea-smoothed Spanish bones onto the sand dunes.

The few Armada crewmen who staggered ashore alive were likely to meet an equally gruesome end. The English garrisons that girded the countryside had only sketchy and infrequent reports from London to tell them of the Armada's progress. Terrified that the bedraggled cast-aways were in fact the first wave of a full Spanish invasion, they reacted with a nervous blood-frenzy, rounding up and slaughtering whatever Spaniards they could find. "Since it hath pleased God by His hand upon the rocks to drown the greater and better sort of them," wrote Sir William Fitzwilliam, Elizabeth's Lord Deputy in Ireland, "I will, with His favor, be His soldier for the dispatching of those ragges which yet remain." A number of Irishmen served in the Queen's pay and were happy to help. One of them, Melaghlin McCabb, boasted of having personally slain 80 Spaniards.

Some of the Spaniards clung to survival with a fierce and stubborn courage. Consider the odyssey of Alonso de Leiva, the flaxen-haired chevalier who had commanded the Armada's rear guard during the Channel fights. Leiva was responsible for the 820-ton carrack *Rata Santa María Encoronada* and her company: 335 soldiers, 84 crewmen and, most particularly, some 60 aristocratic comrades-in-arms—young hidalgos who had brought along squads of servants, chests of finery and all manner of other paraphernalia for proper campaigning. Leiva had led the *Rata* into the center of every Armada skirmish, and she had been hit repeatedly by gunshot. The Atlantic storms in early September completed her ravagement.

On September 10, sighting the Irish coast at Erris Head on the massive westward bulge of County Mayo, Leiva decided to head for the land. He felt his way south, past a nasty archipelago of shoals and islets, and rounded up into the shelter of Blacksod Bay. There are several fine, protected anchorages in Blacksod Bay; Leiva's pilot chose the worst. The carrack was no sooner anchored than the entering tide surged past and dragged her onto the beach, where successive tides dug her irrevocably into the sand.

No one lost his life in the grounding, and much of the ship's armament and rich cargo was carried safely ashore. But Leiva and the 479 men he led had lost their transportation back to Spain.

Leiva was not a man to bemoan outrageous fortune. He quickly busied the stranded men at setting up camp in a ruined fortress near the beach, so that they could defend themselves if the English should attack. They then began scouring the countryside for food—and for news of other Spanish ships.

As luck would have it, another Spanish vessel had in fact anchored nearby. She was the *Duquesa Santa Ana*, the 900-ton West India merchantman that the *Rata* had helped rescue one morning in the Channel from an attack by Hawkins. The *Duquesa Santa Ana* had put in at a sheltered cove across Blacksod Bay, and Leiva marched his troop of hidalgos and soldiers around to her. The merchantman was already overcrowded, with more than 300 men of her own and some refugees she had picked up from another sinking ship, but seeing his countrymen in distress, the captain agreed to take all of Leiva's company aboard his vessel and transport them.

The nearest Spanish port was some 800 miles to the south, against the prevailing winds. With the extraordinary load she was now committed to carry, the *Duquesa Santa Ana* would clearly never reach it. Her captain and Leiva conferred, and decided to head north for Scotland, the closest neutral territory. Scotland was only 200 miles away, and presumably downwind. There they might obtain provisions and, if luck was with them, a vessel to take some of the additional passengers off their hands.

The *Duquesa Santa Ana* eased out of Blacksod Bay and into the Atlantic. She steered north past the string of shoals by Erris Head, across the 50-mile sweep of Donegal Bay, and on toward Bloody Foreland. Before reaching it she was struck by a set of westerly squalls. The winds drove her east, toward shore, until she could no longer fetch the next point. An anchor was dropped, the cable parted, and the *Duquesa Santa Ana* was dashed upon the beach.

Leiva's second shipwreck proved to be considerably more disastrous than his first. A wild sea was breaking, the shoreline presented an obstacle course of sand and rock, and men drowned in great numbers. Leiva broke his leg on the capstan and had to be carried. Crippled though he was, he took charge of the survivors. Once again defenses were set up in a nearby abandoned fortress. Again scouts went out in search of provi-

Seventeenth Century English playing cards recount the demise of the Armada in self-congratulatory words and pictures. Pointedly, Catholic clergymen turn up on the cards designated as knaves.

Arthur L.ᵈ Grey, S.ʳ Francis Knolles, S.ʳ Iohn Norris, S.ʳ Richard Bingham, S.ʳ Rog Williams & others in a Councell of War, consulting how y.ᵉ land Service should be Ordered

The Spaniards on sight of the Fireships weighing Ancors cutting Cables and betakeing themselves to flight w.ᵗʰ a hideousе noise & in great Confusion.

Severall Iesuits hang'd for Treason against the Queene and for having a hand in the Invasion —

sions and assistance. And again a report came back of another Spanish vessel stranded in the vicinity.

This third ship was the galleass *Girona*, which had run into Killybegs in Donegal Bay, some 20 rugged cross-country miles to the south. A friendly Irish chieftain pointed the way across the 1,000-foot uplands toward Killybegs. The Spaniards labored up the heather-flocked ridges through an uncomfortable autumn drizzle. Leiva, who was still immobilized by his leg wound, rode in an improvised litter carried by four soldiers. When they reached Killybegs, they found the *Girona* riding at anchor with a broken rudder. The wreckage of two other Armada vessels lay beached nearby.

Leiva assessed the situation and took firm command once again. The two wrecks were cannibalized of timber and cordage to rebuild the *Girona*'s rudder and to replace her frayed rigging and shot-through timbers. Another chieftain, a leader of the powerful O'Donnell clan, offered the Spaniards aid and hospitality. After three weeks of repair work, the *Girona* was pronounced ready to sail again. On the 26th of October, shortly before sunrise, the galleass slipped out of Killybegs on a full ebb tide.

The *Girona* now carried the combined survivors of five shipwrecks. In addition to her own complement of soldiers, mariners and oarsmen, there were Leiva's group from the *Rata* and the *Duquesa Santa Ana*, plus men from the cannibalized wrecks—perhaps 1,300 souls in all, aboard a vessel that was designed to accommodate no more than 600. But with a fair wind up the Irish coast, her passage seemed easy

More then halfe y' Spanish Fleet Taken and Sunck

The Spanish Ships lost on the Coast of Scotland and 700 Souldiers and Marriners cast a Shoare.

The Spanish fleet that remained, returned home difabled & with much dishonom

enough—until the 27th of October, when she bore east toward Scotland. Now the wind shifted north, the seas rose, and the *Girona's* new rudder began to creak and shimmy.

The next afternoon the rudder broke loose entirely. The *Girona* wallowed in the troughs of the mounting seas, out of control. Every wave drove her closer to the ragged northern coast of Ireland. Around midnight she smashed into an enormous corridor of half-submerged rock known as the Giants' Causeway, in County Antrim. She struck the reef sideways, ripped open her bottom, rolled over once and then broke apart. Out spilled cannon, water casks, sea chests, splintered timbers— and bodies. Leiva and his hidalgos, the brightest flowering of Spanish chivalry, were all either crushed or drowned. Of the 1,300 passengers aboard the *Girona*, only nine lived to tell the tale.

The few who survived the inhuman hardships and frustrations of the odyssey in Ireland did so by a combination of incorrigible will, unflagging wit—and not a little luck.

One such individual was Captain Francisco de Cuéllar from Segovia. Cuéllar was the kind of naturally picaresque hero who seems destined to weather any difficult situation. As commander of the galleon *San Pedro* during the Armada battles, he was one of the 20 ship captains who had been sentenced to death for desertion at Calais. He managed to fast-talk his way out of a hanging by throwing the blame on his pilot— who, said Cuéllar, had been in charge of the ship while he himself lay in a deep sleep of exhaustion—but he was stripped of his rank and command, and placed in the custody of the fleet's judge advocate, Martín de Aranda. "The judge was very courteous to me," Cuéllar wrote later with smug self-assurance, "because of his great respect for those who are in the right."

The ship on which Cuéllar now sailed—thought to be the *Lavia*, a Levantine carrack—became separated from the main fleet somewhere northwest of Ireland, along with two other vessels. On September 20 the trio was caught in a storm off Donegal and forced into nearby Sligo Bay. All three ships were hurled onto the beach. "I placed myself on the poop of my ship, having commended myself to God," he wrote, "and from thence I gazed at a terrible spectacle. Many were drowning in the ships, others, casting themselves into the water, sank to the bottom without returning to the surface." Cuéllar went on to say that he saw "others on rafts and barrels, and gentlemen on pieces of timber; others cried out aloud in the ships, calling upon God."

Cuéllar himself could not decide what to do. He could not swim, and if he jumped into the sea he would probably drown. For that matter, the shore was not much more inviting than the surf, because, he reflected, it was "full of enemies, who went about jumping and dancing with delight at our misfortunes; and when any of our people reached the beach two hundred savages and other enemies stripped him until he was left in his naked skin."

While Cuéllar pondered, a large hatch cover came floating by and he decided to snag it. Being a generous soul, he called out to the judge advocate, his designated jailer, who was cowering nearby, "very sorrowful and depressed," and offered to share his find. The worthy judge had stuffed a quantity of heavy gold crowns into his doublet and hose, and was considerably encumbered by their weight; only with difficulty did Cuéllar get him onto the improvised raft. His efforts were in vain. "In casting off from the ship," Cuéllar wrote, "there came a huge wave breaking over us in such manner that the judge was unable to resist it, and the wave bore him away and drowned him as he cried out, calling upon God. I could not aid him as the hatchway cover, being without weight at one end, began to turn over with me and at that moment a piece of timber crushed my legs."

Moments later Cuéllar found himself on the beach, "without knowing how" he got there, covered with blood from the injury to his legs. All around him the Irish brigands, with blood-chilling whoops and cries, were working over the bodies of his countrymen. The captain crawled up the sand and hid in a stand of marsh grass. Sometime after dusk he was joined by another Spaniard, "a very nice young fellow, quite naked, so dazed he could not speak, not even to tell me who he was." The two men lay quiet, half-dead from pain and hunger and cold, listening to the sounds of pillage along the shoreline. A short while later they faced another threat; soldiers from a nearby English garrison rode up and began rounding up whatever Spaniards they could find. Cuéllar managed to stay in hiding, however.

After perhaps half an hour, he heard the sound of footsteps. He looked up to see the menacing forms of two Irishmen, one of whom was carrying a large ax. Cuéllar froze. Surely his hour had come. Then a strange thing happened. "They were grieved to see us," the captain wrote later, "and without speaking a word to us, they cut a quantity of rushes and grass, and covered us well; and then betook themselves to the shore to plunder."

Cuéllar dozed off, and awoke shortly before daybreak. He nudged the man who was lying next to him, but got no response. The man was dead. As the sun rose all was quiet, and the captain decided it would be safe to move inland. He struggled to his feet and limped off. Some distance down the road he came upon a small monastery. "I found it deserted and the church and images of the saints burned and completely ruined, and twelve Spaniards hanging within the church by the act of the Lutheran English," he wrote later. "All the monks had fled to the woods for fear of the enemy, who would have sacrificed them as well if they had caught them."

No help there. Cuéllar walked on. After a day or two he spotted a hamlet of thatched huts across the downs and made for it. Suddenly four figures leaped out from behind some rocks. "An old savage of more than seventy years came out, and two armed young men—one English, the other French—and a girl age twenty, most beautiful," Cuéllar continued. "They were all going to the shore to plunder.

"The Englishman came up, saying, 'Yield, Spanish poltroon,' and made a slash at me with a knife, desiring to kill me. I parried the blow with a stick I was carrying, but in the end he got me, cutting the sinew of my right leg. He tried to repeat the blow."

Just in time, the beautiful colleen stepped in to grab the Englishman's arm. She then fell to with her companions to strip Cuéllar of all of his possessions. In addition to some money and a gold chain, the assailants took a pouch of treasured religious relics, which "the young savage woman hung about her neck, telling me that she was a Christian"—an assertion that Cuéllar found bizarre in a person of such alien ways. They then retreated to their huts with their loot. But as the captain lay by the roadside, nursing his gashed leg, the colleen sent him a poultice of herbs, some oatcakes for dinner, as well as directions to the next village.

And so Captain Cuéllar limped on through the bogs and brambles of Ireland. For upward of four wintry months he wandered about, dodging English patrols, begging food and shelter, and suffering the whims— and unexpected kindnesses—of the country's uncouth inhabitants. He was robbed again, this time of every last stitch of clothing, and he had nothing to cover his nakedness with but a mat of straw and bracken. Later he stumbled into a hut where the occupant spoke to him in Latin, and clad and fed him. In another village he was taken captive by the blacksmith, and spent a week of forced labor stoking the forge before he could make his escape.

At one point Cuéllar found asylum with an Irish chieftain, Brian O'Rourke, "an important savage very friendly to the King of Spain," who had already taken some 70 other Armada refugees under his wing. On receiving news that a Spanish ship had anchored up the coast and was taking on passengers, the group left en masse to seek it out. Cuéllar started with them, but he had to turn back because of his leg wound. He was lucky. The ship hit a reef shortly after sailing and went down with the loss of all hands.

For several months Cuéllar sheltered with another chieftain, Dartry MacClancy, in a stone bastion in some marshes near Sligo Bay. He lived in reasonable security, "acting as a real savage like themselves," while his wounds healed and his strength returned. He was nursed by the chieftain's wife, whom he found "beautiful in the extreme"—indeed, to Cuéllar no Irish female seemed otherwise. The captain reciprocated with long tales of life in Spain, and gypsy-style palm readings.

In December this idyll was cut short by the English infantry, which marched overland from Dublin to lay siege to MacClancy's castle. Mac-Clancy and his clansmen withdrew into the hills, but Cuéllar decided to stay. Eight other Armada refugees were also lodged in the castle, and together they decided to defend it. For 17 days the Spaniards held out, with six muskets and six crossbows among them, while the attackers wallowed about in the freezing bogs outside. Finally the English gave up and marched back to Dublin. MacClancy returned, delighted to find his castle intact. Hoping to attach the resourceful Cuéllar permanently to his household, he offered his sister's hand in marriage. Cuéllar politely declined. The time had come to move on once again. But he went with some grateful recollections.

"These savages liked us well," he wrote, "and indeed if they had not taken as much care of us as they did of themselves, not one of us would still be alive."

Eventually Cuéllar reached Scotland, where he stayed six months,

In the candlelit chapel deep in El Escorial, two troubled
courtiers and a priest stand watch as King Philip kneels in prayer
after learning the fate of the Armada. The aging monarch
had no sooner absorbed the news of the debacle than he busied
himself with plans for another invasion of England.

begging food and shelter, until he could find passage to Flanders. At the end of September 1589, he embarked with a crowd of Armada refugees in a convoy of four merchantmen.

By now, a year and a half had passed since King Philip's noble fleet had sailed so proudly out of Lisbon, and the final results of the Enterprise of England were all too plain. Every squadron had lost at least one ship. The urcas and the Mediterranean merchantmen—not designed to weather a stormy Atlantic passage—had suffered enormously; seven urcas and 16 merchantmen were wrecked. Of the 130 vessels that had set their helms toward England, not more than 60 returned to Spain. The toll in personnel was even more hideous. Out of 29,000 soldiers and mariners and officers and gentlemen-adventurers, as many as two thirds had perished—if not from gunshot or shipwreck, then from disease, starvation and exposure. "There was no famous or worthy family in all Spaine," one scribe concluded, that "lost not a son, a brother or a kinsman" to the Enterprise of England.

The surviving ships presented a sorry spectacle as they staggered into various Spanish ports along the Bay of Biscay. They began appearing during the last weeks of September 1588—the same period that had brought such catastrophe to the stragglers off Ireland. Medina Sidonia led with the *San Martín*. Nearly half his soldiers and crew, some 180 men, had already died of scurvy, typhus and influenza, and more were dropping each day. Medina Sidonia himself was exhausted and semi-delirious with fever.

The ships were as badly off as the men. The purser Calderón, aboard the *San Salvador*, recalled that for the last three days before dropping anchor at Santander on September 23—while he and his shipmates went without drinking water—the bilge pumps were barely able to keep pace with the sea water flooding into the hold. Many other returning ships were too crippled ever to sail again.

Every vessel seemed to endure special tortures. On some of the ships, men died of starvation or thirst within sight of the coast of Spain. One ship ran aground in harbor because no crewman could muster the strength to lower the sails or drop the anchor. Up the coast at Corunna, Juan Martínez de Recalde, vice admiral of the Enterprise and Spain's finest seaman, conned his *San Juan* into harbor, carrying survivors from another vessel that had foundered in Blasket Sound. Then he fell dead of exhaustion. And at San Salvador to the east, the dashing Miguel de Oquendo, who had been in the thick of every major battle throughout the decade, was carried ashore in the last throes of typhus. As he lay dying, an accidental fire sprang up in the magazine of his flagship, the *Santa Ana*, and she burned at anchor with the loss of 100 lives.

As the full news of the disaster penetrated the hushed chambers of El Escorial, Philip digested it with the imperturbable stoicism that was his nature. The King was now a tired, aging man, crippled by gout, his beard whitening and his complexion fading to a chalky pallor. Nonetheless, he took quick and compassionate action. Hospitals were set up to attend the sick. Pensions were established for widows and orphans. A Mass of Thanksgiving was ordered for the men who had returned, and a Requi-

A medallion cast soon after the event commemorates England's victory over the Armada. One side bears a portrait of the Queen and a Latin inscription trumpeting her worldly riches; the other has a bay tree—symbol of hardiness —withstanding a bolt of lightning, and the legend "Not even dangers affect it."

Queen Elizabeth rests a possessive hand on the globe as she sits between two pictures celebrating heaven-sent winds that were believed to have filled the sails of her own fleet while simultaneously dashing the Spaniards' ships on the rocks.

em sung for those who had not. All Spain was blaming Medina Sidonia for the Armada's failure: "If only Santa Cruz or Recalde or Oquendo or Pedro de Valdés had been in command, everything would have turned out differently," one chronicler mourned. But the King showed Medina Sidonia a statesmanly forgiveness. He absolved the Duke of further obligation and sent him quietly home in a curtained horse litter, to live out his days among the orange groves at Sanlúcar. The only high-ranking officer to earn royal censure was Diego Flores de Valdés, who for general orneriness and incompetence was briefly jailed.

Historians of later years, seeking to wring poignancy from the Armada's defeat, have embellished the story of Philip's reaction. In one account the King, after praying in his chapel at El Escorial, swept up a silver candlestick from the altar and vowed to melt it down to help pay

Valiant finale for the "Revenge"

In this tapestry depiction of the last action of the Revenge, enemy galleons converge on the English warship as her toppled foremast bobs in the water before her.

If ever a ship could be said to symbolize the gallant spirit that defended Elizabethan England, it was the *Revenge*. Francis Drake won lasting fame for the galleon when he took her on a chase after the *Nuestra Señora del Rosario* and bagged the first—and, as it proved, the richest—prize of the encounter with the Armada. But an even greater luster would accrue to her on a subsequent mission.

In the three years that followed the Armada's defeat, the *Revenge* was assigned to routine patrols in European waters. Then came a challenge worthy of her past. In the spring of 1591, she sailed to the Azores as part of a small fleet of six warships and a few supply vessels under Lord Thomas Howard, a nephew of the great admiral who had commanded the English against the Armada. The mission was to intercept Spanish treasure ships returning from the coast of India; such ships sailed annually in convoys, and sometimes a single vessel might carry a cargo worth more than £100,000.

For six months the *Revenge* and her companion ships waited in vain, their bottoms fouling, their men sickening. Finally, on August 30, scouts reported that the Spanish treasure was on the way, but it was escorted by an enormous fleet. Some 53 ships were bearing down. Many of them were galleons, all of them heavily gunned and crowded with soldiers. Having little taste for hopeless combat, Lord Howard gave the order for the fleet to set sail for home.

On board the *Revenge* was Vice Admiral Sir Richard Grenville, a member of Parliament, shipowner and sometime warrior. In 1567 he had joined a campaign to rout the Turks from eastern Europe; in the 1580s he made two trips to the New World; and in 1588 he contributed three ships to the fleet that fought the Armada. Even more than most Englishmen of the day, Grenville nourished a virulent hatred for Spaniards. According to legend, tales of their cruelty drove him to such rage that he would crush drinking glasses with his teeth and swallow the pieces. He welcomed a fight with them under any circumstance—and now took on the 53 enemy ships alone.

Against such odds, the result could hardly have been in doubt. But the *Revenge* put up a spectacular show. First she sank one ship and drove off another. Other ships came close and their men tried to board, but the crew of the *Revenge* held them off—for some 15 hours. By then, her upper works were shot away, the soldiers' pikes were broken and, of the 100 fighting men aboard, 40 were dead and most of the rest were wounded—including Vice Admiral Grenville himself. The captain struck the colors, Grenville was carried to the Spanish flagship to die, and the *Revenge* was taken in tow as a Spanish prize.

Five days later, what enemy guns had failed to do, wind and sea accomplished; a fierce storm arose and sent the *Revenge* to the bottom, sparing her the indignity of serving under an enemy flag. Grenville could have been speaking for his ship as well as himself when he uttered his last words: "I have ended my life as a true soldier ought to do that hath fought for his country, queen, religion and honor."

for another fleet. "I sent my ships to fight against men," he is supposed to have said, "and not against the winds and waves of God." Such petulance toward the Almighty was not in Philip's character. His true reaction to the failed expedition showed greater humility and forbearance. "The uncertainty of naval enterprises is well known," he wrote his archbishops. "We are bound to praise God for all things that He is pleased to do." The King then turned his mind to all the other ever-pressing concerns of God and Empire.

In England, it finally dawned upon Elizabeth and her ministers in September that the Armada landings in Ireland did not mean an invasion, but a rout. A great victory had been won, glorious and resounding beyond anyone's hopes, and the nation exploded into a bacchanal of self-congratulation. Bonfires leaped from street corners, balladeers sang paeans, and the chroniclers recorded the great event as told to them by the participants. The Spaniards' "invincible and dreadful navy, with all its great and terrible ostentation," one of them quoted Drake as saying, "did not in all their sailing about England so much as sink or take one ship, bark, pinnance or cockboat of ours, or even burn so much as one sheepcote on this land." Silver coins were issued, both in England and in the Netherlands, commemorating the triumph. One coin proclaimed, *"Flavit deus et dissipati sunt,"* ("God breathed and they were scattered")—a pious reference to the storms off Ireland, which many people believed had been the principal cause of victory.

The Armada's dispersal happened to coincide with the 30th anniversary of Elizabeth's coronation, and on December 10 she celebrated both events in a lavish thanksgiving service at St. Paul's Cathedral. A triumphal procession "imitating the ancient Romans," said a scribe, moved through London, the Queen riding in a canopied chariot drawn by two white horses, and trailed by mounted regiments of peers, judges, generals and other notables. City militiamen in scarlet liveries stood braced on either side of the parade route, which was draped in blue bunting, while banners and ensigns fluttered overhead. At the cathedral, Elizabeth listened to a sermon that praised God's wisdom in siding with the English. She then sat back to enjoy an anthem, the words of which she had composed herself, exulting: "He made the winds and waters rise / To scatter all mine enemies."

Again, the winds of God—a persistent emphasis that gave credit to fate at the expense of human ingenuity. Somehow the expert gunnery and seamanship of Howard, Drake and Hawkins had been forgotten in the excitement. No matter; the fact remained that England had been saved, by whatever means. The eminent Richard Hakluyt, Elizabethan editor of nautical narratives, summed up the matter well enough. The "magnificent, huge and mighty fleet of the Spaniards," he wrote, "in the yeere 1588 vanished into smoake; to the great confusion and discouragement of the authors thereof."

Hostilities between England and Spain did not come to an end with the Armada's defeat. War continued, off and on, for another 16 years. There were hard-fought encounters in the Caribbean, in the Azores, along the Iberian coast and in Ireland. Both sides saw moments of high brilliance and valor, and also some fair-sized fiascos. In 1589, for example, Elizabeth launched an armada of her own: 126 ships and 21,000 men under the command of Francis Drake, with orders to smash the remnants of Philip's fleet at Santander. Drake returned home with a disappointing £30,000 in prizes, his ships severely damaged by storm, half his men stricken with dysentery and typhus—and the backbone of Spanish sea power still unbroken.

Spain had begun to pick up the pieces of its battered fleet and rebuild as soon as the results of the Armada were known. Within a few years the Spanish navy was as strong as it had ever been. The Indies plate fleets continued to sail home unharmed, even though the English tried to stop them with a blockade of the Azores. In 1591, a Spanish fleet surprised the blockading squadron, and so achieved its country's most satisfying triumph. The English admiral wisely fled. But one captain, sailing in Drake's old *Revenge*, stayed to fight—alone. It was a glorious gesture, and thoroughly futile. England's most famous and dreaded warship was blasted to bits.

Philip never gave up the idea of invading England. In late 1596 he sent a second armada, 100 ships strong, toward the English Channel. It had no better luck than the first. Near the Bay of Biscay a violent storm blew up, worse than anything in 1588, and more than half the fleet was destroyed. Nothing daunted, the King tried again the next year. Again a storm struck, this time 20 miles south of the Lizard, and the third armada was driven back to Spain. If ever the winds of God blew foul for King Philip, it was during these two attempts.

A fourth and final armada, in 1601, achieved an objective of sorts. Some 5,000 soldiers landed in Kinsale on the southern coast of Ireland, in support of a rebellion by two Irish chieftains. The Spanish troops held their ground for three months until they were forced to surrender to a more powerful English army under Lord Mountjoy and Sir George Carew. With a fine-tuned chivalry not always shared by his contemporaries, Carew sent the Spaniards home, without ransom or reprisals. The following year, the grateful Spanish general sent him a crate of wine and oranges.

And so the war continued. It outlasted Drake and Hawkins, both of whom died of fever during an expedition to the West Indies in the winter of 1595-1596. It continued through the death of Philip in 1598, and past the death of Elizabeth five years later. It limped along toward the end in general weariness and inattention, until James I of England and Philip III of Spain officially brought it to a close with the signing of the Treaty of Westminster in 1604.

The conflict had been strangely inconclusive. No territory changed hands. The balance of military power did not significantly shift. Neither side gained dominance over the seas. Yet something of lasting importance did happen, and it happened during those first two weeks of gunfire in the English Channel in 1588. The reverberation of the guns, and the image of that great Spanish fleet fleeing north, settled in men's minds and would not leave. It glowed bright for the Protestant Dutch as they continued to defy the Duke of Parma's occupation troops, fighting their way to a truce with Spain in 1609, and eventually to independence.

English warships swarm into Cádiz harbor in 1596 and overwhelm a force of Spanish galleys (background, center). In a struggle lasting for more than a decade after the defeat of the Armada, England hurled several such expeditions against Spain—holding off other armadas and eventually outclassing Spain as the world's preeminent maritime nation.

It took on a golden nostalgic sheen for the seafaring English as, years later, they sipped their port and talked of glories past and to come. Until that moment Spain, the world's first global empire, had marched from crusade to victorious crusade until it seemed unstoppable. Now Spain's advance had been abruptly halted. Spanish power lasted another half century; Spanish prestige never recovered.

The Armada battles also changed the nature of war at sea. For the first time in history, a naval battle had been fought by ships and guns alone, rather than by the ancient practice of grappling and boarding, and hand-to-hand swordplay. "To clap two ships together without consideration belongs rather to a madman than to a man of war," wrote Sir Walter Raleigh a few years later, and his remark was prophetic. For 1588 brought in a new naval era, based on speed, maneuverability and firepower, that would last more than three centuries, until the age of the submarine and the aircraft carrier.

Residuum of the Armada's last ordeal

For nearly 400 years, the 20-odd Spanish vessels that came to grief on the coast of Ireland lay almost undisturbed in their ocean graves. Periodically they gave off ghostly reminders of their presence—as when gold coins washed up on the beach here and there. But no serious effort was made to test their promise of treasure until the 1960s, when a Belgian archeologist and diver named Robert Sténuit embarked on a hunt for the lost galleass Girona.

Sténuit began by spending long hours in the libraries of Brussels, Madrid, Paris and London, poring over accounts of the Girona's demise. Having narrowed his search to the coast of County Antrim in Northern Ireland, he set off in June 1967 for Portballintrae, a fishing village 50 miles north of Belfast, and the site of many a shipwreck. The 400-foot cliffs that loom nearby are "sheer and terrifying," Sténuit later wrote; they "call for death and cry out for tragedy."

An ordinary tourist's guidebook for the area provided a tantalizing clue: A cove near the village bore the name Port na Spaniagh, Gaelic for "Spanish Point." Sténuit resolved to make his first dive there. He had no sooner touched bottom than he spotted a 27-inch ingot of lead with five crosses stamped on its face, marking it as ballast of Spanish manufacture. Swimming on through a corridor of rocks, he found a bronze cannon and its powder chamber. "A Spanish Armada gun!" he thought. "There wasn't a museum in the world that had one."

More investigation showed the cove held tons of naval and military equipment, fragments of cooking pots for everyday living, and personal luxuries such as gold buttons. Some of the objects had been damaged by corrosion or the sea's buffeting, but many items, once freed from a chalky encrustation of lime, were found to be in perfect condition.

Inevitably, the dazzling find lured other marine archeologists to the Irish coast, and within four years the remains of the galleons Trinidad Valencera and Santa María de la Rosa had been located to the north and the west. Along with some of Sténuit's trove, a sampling of the objects they yielded appears here and on the following pages, set against 19th Century engravings of the Armada vessels in their death throes on the rocks of Ireland.

50-POUNDER BRONZE CANNON

1½- TO 2½-INCH IRON SHOT

6- TO 10-INCH IRON AND STONE CANNON SHOT

BRONZE ASTROLABE— MISSING ITS POINTER

BRASS NAVIGATIONAL DIVIDERS

MUSKET STOCK AND RAMROD

DAGGER HILT AND SHEATH

Echoes of shipboard life

As they plunged from the shattered ships, the Armada's goods and chattels settled helter-skelter on the ocean floor, presenting 20th Century divers with a variety of unexpected finds that ranged from exquisite silver candlesticks to foul-smelling lentils moldering in a pottery jar. Despite the disorder, the spilled treasures generated an almost palpable sense of human presence. The pewter plate shown opposite, for example, was engraved on the underside of the rim with the name Matute; it was a matter of public record that a man named Francisco Ruiz Matute had been aboard the galleon *Santa María de la Rosa* as commander of the Sicilian infantry.

A light note was provided by another find—a pair of cups used in some kind of game of chance, perhaps tossing dice. Medina Sidonia's orders to the fleet strictly forbade gambling; but clearly some men disported themselves as they pleased when the commander was looking the other way.

COPPER BUCKET

SILVER CANDLESTICKS

WOODEN GAMING CUPS

WOODEN BOWL AND SPOON

SILVER TABLE FORKS

PEWTER PLATE

BLACKSMITH'S HAMMER HEADS

SURGEON'S BRONZE MORTAR

POTTERY RATION JAR

Possessions that tell the tale of loss

The wreckage that Sténuit and his fellow archeologists retrieved from Irish waters measured the Armada tragedy in countless subtle ways, even through coins. From the remains of the *Girona*, for instance, came a staggering total of 1,267 coins that had been minted in Spain, Portugal, Sicily, Genoa, Mexico and Peru—an indication that no part of Philip II's far-flung domain escaped the loss of men.

More poignant still was the jewelry: crucifixes that professed the faith of the men, chivalric crosses indicating their knighthood, and rings that bespoke their deepest and most private feelings. One small ring was decorated with a hand holding a heart and the inscription *No tengo mas que dar te*— "I have nothing more to give thee." Perhaps it was the parting gift of a sweetheart to her doomed lover on the eve of the expedition in which all of Spain had invested so much.

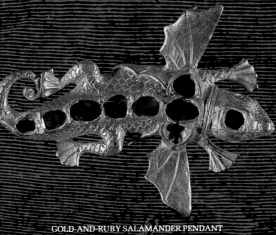

GOLD-AND-RUBY SALAMANDER PENDANT

GOLD RINGS

GOLD MEDALLION

LAPIS LAZULI CAMEO

GOLD CHIVALRIC CROSS

GOLD RELIQUARY

GOLD, DOLPHIN-SHAPED TOOTHPICK

GOLD COINS

SILVER COINS

SILVER CRUCIFIX

GOLD BUTTONS

GOLD CHAINS

Bibliography

Bell, Douglas, *Elizabethan Seamen*. J. B. Lippincott, 1936.

Boynton, Lindsay, *The Elizabethan Militia*. University of Toronto Press, 1967.

Braudel, Fernand, *The Mediterranean and the Mediterranean World in the Age of Philip II* (2 vols.). Harper & Row, 1976.

Camden, William, *The History of the Most Renowned and Victorious Princess Elizabeth, Late Queen of England*. AMS Press, 1970.

Cary, Robert, *Memoirs of Robert Cary, Earl of Monmouth*. Alexander Moring, 1905.

Corbett, Julian S., *Drake and the Tudor Navy* (2 vols.). Longmans, Green, 1899.

Dyer, Florence E., "The Elizabethan Sailorman," *The Mariner's Mirror*, Vol. 10, January 1924. Cambridge University Press.

Fernández Duro, Cesáreo, *La Conquista de las Azores*. Madrid: Est. Tipográfico, 1886.

Fraser, Antonia, *Mary Queen of Scots*. Delacorte Press, 1969.

Froude, James Anthony:
English Seamen in the Sixteenth Century. Charles Scribner's Sons, 1895.
The Spanish Story of the Armada and Other Essays. Charles Scribner's Sons, 1892.

Glasgow, Tom, "Elizabethan Ships Pictured on Smerwick Map, 1580," *The Mariner's Mirror*, Vol. 52, No. 2. Cambridge University Press, 1966.

Graham, Winston, *The Spanish Armadas*. Doubleday, 1972.

Grierson, Edward, *The Fatal Inheritance*. Doubleday, 1969.

Hadfield, A. M., *Time to Finish the Game*. London: Phoenix House, 1964.

Hakluyt, Richard, *Hakluyt's Voyages*. Viking Press, 1965.

Hume, Martin A. S., "Some Survivors of the Armada in Ireland," *Transactions of the Royal Historical Society*, Vol. 11, January 21, 1897. London: Longmans, Green, 1897.

Hume, Martin A. S., ed.:
Calendar of Letters and State Papers (English Affairs), Vol. 4. London: Her Majesty's Stationery Office, 1899.
Calendar of State Papers—Spanish, Vol. 3, 1580-1586. London: Eyre and Spottiswoode, 1896.

Laughton, John Knox, *The Defeat of the Spanish Armada* (2 vols.). Navy Records Society, 1894.

Laughton, John Knox, ed., *State Papers Relating to the Defeat of the Spanish Armada, Anno 1588* (2 vols.). Navy Records Society, 1894.

Lewis, Michael:
The Spanish Armada. Macmillan, 1960.
Armada Guns: A Comparative Study of English and Spanish Armaments. London: George Allen & Unwin, 1961.

Martin, Colin, *Full Fathom Five*. Viking, 1975.

Mattingly, Garrett:
The Armada. Houghton Mifflin, 1959.
The "Invincible" Armada and Elizabethan England. Cornell University Press, 1963.

Merriman, Roger Bigelow, *Philip the Prudent (The Rise of the Spanish Empire in the Old World and in the New)*, Vol. 4. Cooper Square Publishers, 1962.

Motley, John Lothrop, *History of the United Netherlands* (6 vols.). Harper and Brothers, 1900.

Norton, Robert, *The Complete Gunner*. Da Capo Press, 1973.

Oakeshott, Walter, *Founded Upon the Seas*. Books for Libraries Press, 1973.

O'Rahilly, Alfred, *The Massacre at Smerwick*. Cork University Press, 1938.

Padfield, Peter, *Guns at Sea*. St. Martin's Press, 1974.

Parry, John H., *The Establishment of the European Hegemony, 1415-1715*. Harper & Row, 1966.

Pierson, Peter, *Philip II of Spain*. London: Thames and Hudson, 1975.

Pollen, John Hungerford, ed., *Mary Queen of Scots and the Babington Plot*. Edinburgh: University Press, 1922.

Prescott, H. M., *Mary Tudor*. Macmillan, 1953.

Rowse, A. L., *The Expansion of Elizabethan England*. St. Martin's Press, 1955.

Sitwell, Edith, *The Queens and the Hive*. London: Macmillan, 1962.

Stenuit, Robert, *Treasures of the Armada*. E. P. Dutton, 1973.

Thomson, George Malcolm, *Sir Francis Drake*. William Morrow, 1972.

Usherwood, Stephen. *The Great Enterprise*. London: Folio Society, 1978.

Versteeg, Dingman, *The Sea Beggars: Liberators of Holland from the Yoke of Spain*. Continental Publishing, 1901.

Waters, D. W., "The Elizabethan Navy and the Armada Campaign," *The Mariner's Mirror*, Vol. 35, No. 2, April 1949. Cambridge University Press.

Waters, David, *The Art of Navigation in England in Elizabethan and Early Stuart Times*. Hollis and Carter, 1958.

Williams, Neville, *All the Queen's Men*. London: Sphere Books, 1974.

Williamson, James A.:
Hawkins of Plymouth. Barnes & Noble, 1969.
The Age of Drake. London: Adam & Charles Black, 1960.

Woodrooffe, Thomas:
The Enterprise of England. London: Faber and Faber, 1958.
Vantage at Sea. St. Martin's Press, 1958.

Acknowledgments

The index for this book was prepared by Gale Linck Partoyan. The editors wish to thank the following: Gerard J. A. Raven, consultant; John Batchelor, artist, and José María Martínez-Hidalgo y Terán, consultant (pages 82-85); John Batchelor, artist, and John F. Guilmartin Jr., consultant (pages 94-95); Bill Hezlep, artist (page 31); Peter McGinn, artist (endpaper maps); Richard Schlecht, artist, and William Avery Baker, consultant (pages 146-151).

The editors also wish to thank: In Australia: Sydney—The Mitchell Library. In Belgium: Antwerp—Maritime Museum; Brussels—Musée Royaux des Beaux-Arts; Robert Sténuit. In France: Paris—Jean-Pierre Reverseau, Curator, Lionel Dumarche, Librarian, Musée de l'Armée; Marcel Redouté, Curator, Marjolaine Mathikine, Director for Historical Studies, Jacques Chantriot, Researcher, Denise Chaussegroux, Researcher, Catherine Touny, Researcher, Musée de la Marine; Mrs. Hypolite Worms; Calais—Sylvie Renaux, Librarian, Bibliothèque Municipale; Dunkerque—Jacques Kuhnmunch, Curator, Musée de Dunkerque; Versailles—Roland Bossard, Researcher, Musée National des Chateaux de Versailles et de Trianon. In Germany: Berlin—Dr. Roland Klemig, Heidi Klein, Bildarchiv Preussischer Kulturbesitz. In Ireland: Dublin—Desmond Branigan; John de Courcy. In Italy: Rome—Marie Tanner; Florence—Diana Toccafondi-Fantappié, Archivio di Stato. In the Netherlands: Amsterdam—Gemeente Archiefdienst; Rijksmuseum; Rijksmuseum Nederlands Scheepvaart Museum; The Hague—Algemeen Rijksarchief; Koninklijk Kabinet van Munten, Penningen en Gesneden Stenen; Martin de Vries, Photographer; Leyden—Leyden University Library; Stedelijk Museum de Lakenhal; Middleburg—Zeeuws Museum; Rotterdam—Atlas van Stolk. In Portugal: Lisbon—Rainer Daehnhardt, President of the Portuguese Society of Antique Arms. In Spain: Madrid—Hipólito Escolar, Director, Manuel Carrión, Sub-Director, Biblioteca Nacional; The Count of Revillagigedo; Fermín Muñoz, Secretary to the Duchess of Alba, Liria Palace; Guillermo de Mulder; Colonel Antonio Galvís Loriga, Secretary General, Museo del Ejército; Jaime Jiménez, Museo Naval; Fernando Fuertes de Villavicencio, Consejero Delegado Gerente, Patrimonio Nacional; Pilar Lopez-Brea, Directora de la Biblioteca, Real Academia de Historia; Barcelona—Laurean Carbonell, Curator, Museo Marítimo, Reales Atarazanas; El Escorial—Eusebio Sáez, Assistant Administrator, Fathers Alonso and Teodoro, Librarians, Palacio de el Escorial; Sanlúcar de Barrameda—The Duchess of Medina Sidonia; Seville—Professor Francisco Morales Padrón, Professor of Geographical Discovery, University of Seville; Valladolid—Armando Represa, Director, Archivo de Simancas. In the United Kingdom: London—Marjorie Willis, BBC Hulton Picture Library; Clare Austin, Department of Manuscripts, British Library; R. Gardner, K. R. Miller, Department of Coins and Medals, R. T. Williams, Department of Prints and Drawings, British Museum; Pat Blackett, Jane Dacey, Ian Friel, P. R. Ince,

David Lyon, P. T. van der Merwe, Joan Moore, Rena Prentice, Roger Quarm, J. E. Tucker, National Maritime Museum; Mrs. S. Barter Bailey, Mr. H. L. Blackmore, H. M. Tower of London; Department of Textiles, Victoria and Albert Museum; Belfast—Laurence N. W. Flanagan, John Kelly, Ulster Museum; Edinburgh—Sheila Gill, Scottish National Portrait Gallery; Plymouth—Maureen V. Attrill, James Barber, Plymouth City Museum and Art Gallery; St. Andrews—Colin Martin, University of St. Andrews.

The editors also wish to thank: In the United States: Alexandria, Virginia—Marilyn Murphy; New York, New York—Laura Lane, Marian Weston, Picture Li-

brary, American Heritage; Sheila Curl, Rare Book Division, Gerald Alexander, Map Division, Spencer Collection, New York Public Library; Providence, Rhode Island—C. Danial Elliott, Bibliographical Assistant, The John Carter Brown Library, Brown University; Silver Spring, Maryland—Sigrid Bloch; Worcester, Massachusetts—Richard Ford, Director, The John Woodman Higgins Armory Museum.

Valuable sources of quotations were *The Defeat of the Spanish Armada* by John Knox Laughton, Navy Records Society, 1894; *The Armada* by Garrett Mattingly, Houghton Mifflin, 1959; and *The Enterprise of England* by Thomas Woodrooffe, London: Faber and Faber, 1958.

Picture Credits

174

Index